TRACING YOUR YOUR
SECOND WORLD WAR
ANCESTORS

— SIMON FOWLER —

First published 2006
© Simon Fowler 2006

All rights reserved. No reproduction
permitted without prior permission
of the publisher:

COUNTRYSIDE BOOKS
3 Catherine Road
Newbury, Berkshire

To view our complete range of books,
please visit us at
www.countrysidebooks.co.uk

ISBN 1 85306 936 1
EAN 978 1 85306 936 9

Designed by Peter Davies, Nautilus Design

Produced through MRM Associates Ltd., Reading
Typeset by Techniset Typesetters, Newton-le-Willows
Printed by Woolnough Bookbinding Ltd., Irthlingborough

ESSEX COUNTY
COUNCIL LIBRARY

CONTENTS

INTRODUCTION

Even after nearly 70 years the Second World War is still an immensely popular subject. Hundreds of books are published each year and TV programmers know that shows about the war are sure to have high ratings. Indeed, several satellite channels seem to show nothing but repeats of these programmes. And the rapidly declining numbers of veterans are becoming folk heroes in the way that the veterans of the First World War were a decade or so ago.

This is largely, but not entirely, an Anglo-Saxon phenomenon. Compared with the Germans and Russians, let alone the peoples of occupied Europe and Asia, the British, Americans and their Commonwealth allies had a 'good' war. We had our setbacks, but in the end right triumphed. And unlike the Great War, the Second World War was clearly a war of good versus evil.

Certainly this is what I learned as a child by listening to stories of the war. Even if my immediate family did nothing heroic, the fathers of my friends all seemed to have been war heroes (at least in the eyes of their children). Yet, my father occasionally told me about his time as a radiographer at King's College Hospital in South London as a firewatcher and how he once had to x-ray the survivors of the V2 bomb which fell on Woolworths at New Cross in November 1944. My mother grew up in a Jewish family near Breslau (now Wroclaw) in Silesia. At the age of 18 she was on the last boat from Germany that was taking parties of refugees to Palestine: she was to become a children's nurse. But on the outbreak of war the ship docked at Dover and she found employment at the local hospital. It was strange to find her aliens' entry document at The National Archives and extremely disturbing when I recently discovered what happened to her parents, on an Israeli website listing Holocaust victims.

Stanley Tiquet, It Happened Here: The Story of Civil Defence in Wanstead and Woodford 1939-1945 *(Borough Council of Wanstead and Woodford, 1948).*

This book is designed to help you research the war for yourself. Inevitably there is a bias towards family historians researching fathers and grandfathers who served in the forces, for genealogists make up the vast majority of visitors to archives, but people interested in other aspects of the war may also find it useful.

There is still a myth that it is impossible to find anything out about the war. Indeed, a very eminent family historian, who should have known better, recently told me this. The main genealogical problem is that service and medal records are still with the Ministry of Defence, although there are occasional rumours that some medal records are to be transferred to The National Archives at Kew. But it will be at least a decade before any service records are released.

With the exception of intelligence material, virtually every important historical record relating to the Second World War has been opened to public inspection, although much ephemeral material has been destroyed. With the advent of the internet, it has also become much easier to find out which records are to be found where. Normally the first port of call will be The National Archives (TNA), formerly the Public Record Office, at Kew, but there are scores of other archives, libraries and museums which might also have material.

This book assumes no prior knowledge of military history or of archives themselves. The whole point is to encourage you, the reader, to get out of your armchair to do research for yourself. Who knows what you will find?

However, it is not a history of the war itself. There are a large number of excellent general histories and more specialist accounts. See the bibliography and individual chapters for a number of suggestions.

As always I am grateful for the encouragement of Nicholas Battle, Paula Leigh and their team at Countryside Books in writing this book. Over the years students at family history classes and lectures, together with letters from readers of *Family History Monthly* and *Ancestors*, have raised questions, some of which are answered here. I'd also like to thank Sylvia for meals and some perceptive proofreading as well as Mike Booker for photographs of El Alamein. Errors and omissions are, of course, my own.

Simon Fowler

1

GETTING STARTED

Although the Second World War is beginning to fade into memory it continues to fascinate historians – professional and amateur alike. Because it is so relatively recent it is sometimes thought that the records are still closed, particularly relating to individuals. Initially this can be a blow, as most people are drawn to the subject by a desire to find out what happened to an individual, often a parent or grandparent during their military service, or are moved by the names on a local war memorial and want to know more about these people. However, there are a huge number of resources available, which make up for the fact that, for the most part, service documents and personnel records in general are closed except to veterans and their next of kin. The purpose of this book is to show you where and how to start your research and to discuss the sources which are available. In other words, it's a technical manual to help you begin to research the war for yourself and to provide answers to some of the questions you may come across in the course of your investigations.

WHERE TO START

The best place to begin your research is to work out what you know already. Write down definite facts as well as anything that you are not absolutely sure of. Of course, it is pretty important to know which service (Army, Royal Navy, Royal Air Force) he or she was with. It is also very useful to have to hand:

- the full name of the person you are researching, as well as any variants of which you might be aware. Your father, known as Tommy Atkins, might have enlisted as John Thomas Atkins or be in the records as T. J. Atkins, or even have the name misspelt by the clerks as James Atkens

- which unit he served with; that is, regiment or corps for the Army, ship(s) in the Royal Navy, and squadron in the Royal Air Force
- when he served and when he was discharged
- date of death if killed in action or died of wounds
- where he served – in the United Kingdom, or overseas. The Second World War was a global war and British and Commonwealth servicemen and women found themselves serving around the world from France to French Indo-China via Florida and Freetown.

In an ideal world you would also know:

- his regimental number
- whether injuries or disabilities resulted from his war service. They may have been physical, such as an artificial leg or shrapnel in the body, or psychological, perhaps plaguing him with recurring nightmares
- the medals he was awarded.

This book should help you follow up these leads and give you ideas about where else you might look for information. Once you start, you might be pleasantly surprised about what you can find out.

IDENTIFYING OLD PHOTOGRAPHS

Many families have photographs of men in uniform. With some effort and a bit of luck you should be able to find more about the man and his service from looking carefully at the picture. The first thing to do is to try to identify his regiment from a cap badge or belt buckle. Chevrons on the sleeves of his uniform would indicate that he was a non-commissioned officer, while other patches might denote the number of times he was wounded and the division to which his unit belonged. Over his heart should be the medal ribbons, or possibly the medals themselves. Pips on his shoulder and a smarter cut of uniform would suggest that the sitter is an officer.

However, with the bewildering number of badges, stripes and other insignia it is easy to get confused. Fortunately there are a number of guides to help you identify military uniforms. One of the best (and

A soldier guards a German plane shot down during the Battle of Britain. (Ernest Fairfax, Calling All Arms: the Story of How a Loyal Company of British Men and Women Lived Through Six Historic Years, *Hutchinson, 1945)*

simplest) is Iain Swinnerton, *Identifying your World War I Soldier from Badges and Photographs* (Federation of Family History Societies, 2001). Even though it refers to the First World War most of the insignia continued to be used during the Second World War. Your local library (and more specialist libraries) may have copies of the following books, which can help identify units and uniforms: Jon Mills, *From Scarlet to Khaki: Understanding the Twentieth Century British Military Uniform in Your Family Album* (Wardens Publishing, 2005); Martin Brayley and Richard Ingram, *The World War II Tommy: British Army Uniforms, European Theatre, 1939-45 in Colour Photographs* (Crowood Press, 1998); Howard N. Cole, *Formation Badges of World War 2: Britain, Commonwealth and Empire* (Arms and Armour Press, 1973); Arthur L. Kipling and Hugh L. King, *Head-dress Badges of the British Army: Volume Two: From the End of the Great War to the Present Day* (Frederick Muller, 1979); and Brian L. Davis, *British Army Uniforms and Insignia of World War Two* (Arms and Armour Press, 1983).

An online introduction to the subject can also be found at www.bbc.co.uk/dna/ww2/A1105912. Illustrations of regimental badges (of varying quality) are at www.militarybadges.org.uk/badges/badgestart.htm and the insignia denoting rank at http://www2.powercom.net/-rokats/wwiiuk.html.

BACKGROUND READING

It is also a good idea to familiarise yourself with the period by doing some background reading. A general history of the war will help to put your research into context and provide a backdrop to the events that your person or village went through. Some suggestions are given in Appendix II. There are also hundreds of more specialist books, ranging from accounts of individual regiments or types of aircraft to detailed histories of campaigns, battles or even particular days that can provide more information.

It may be hard to track down some of the more specialist books – most military museums, particularly the National Army Museum, RAF Museum, and National Maritime Museum should have those mentioned in the text, particularly the ones for their specialism. More generally the Imperial War Museum, British Library and, to a lesser extent, the libraries at The National Archives and Society of Genealogists should have all of the books described.

Firemen extinguish a blaze during the Blitz. (Courtesy of the Imperial War Museum)

If you've got internet access you can find out what is currently in print by visiting the Amazon website (www.amazon.co.uk). An American specialist bookseller, with an excellent website containing some interesting reviews and other material about the war, is Stone and Stone (http://stonebooks.com/archives/040104.shtml).

The British Library Public Catalogue (http://blpc.bl.uk) will supply you with details of virtually every book ever published in Britain. Otherwise you will need to talk to your local library staff (ideally in the reference or local studies section) to see what they can find for you. You can, of course, borrow most books through the inter-library loan service for a small fee.

An increasing amount of information is available on the internet. You will find addresses of websites scattered throughout this book. Apart from official sites, I have included a number of unofficial ones which I felt were serious and reasonably accurate. I have assumed that readers have the internet at home, but if you haven't most libraries have a computer or two linked to the web and there is often training available which will show you how to make the best of the net. Website addresses (URLs) were accurate at the time of going to press, but if you find any which don't work you should be able to find the answer (and related sites) by using a search engine, such as Google (www.google.com).

Research guides produced by The National Archives (TNA) are invaluable, and explain simply what records are available for a particular topic at TNA and, occasionally, elsewhere. They are to be found on TNA's website (www.nationalarchives.gov.uk) – click on the 'Research' menu on the homepage and follow the links. Alternatively, telephone for free copies on 020-8392 5200. They are listed in the appropriate place in the text below.

WHERE THE RECORDS ARE

Books and websites may not be able to answer the queries you have, or stimulate other questions, particularly if you are researching individuals or small units. This means having to look at original material, which may prove to be time-consuming (but deeply addictive and rewarding). Most original documents can be found in one of several places: a national repository or museum, a regimental or service museum, or the local studies library and county record office.

In brief, records of the armed forces and the most important private papers are held at national repositories such as The National Archives (formerly the Public Record Office) and the Imperial War Museum. Regimental and service museums may have archival material relating to their regiment or service, while at local record offices and local studies libraries is material about the locality (such as local government, people and businesses).

There are also a large number of specialist repositories for businesses, universities and charities that may (just possibly) have information. Company archives, for example, may include papers about employees who served in the forces or the provision of a memorial for those who did not return.

Unfortunately there is no hard or fast rule as to who has what, so the papers of a particular commander may be with a local archive or material about a local munitions factory could be at

A number of towns published brief histories of their experiences during the war, which make interesting reading today. The local studies library should have a copy of any such books.

The National Archives. However, the National Register of Archives (www.nra.nationalarchives.gov.uk), maintained by The National Archives at Kew, lists many holdings at local record offices, some museums and specialist repositories. An alternative is the Access to Archives database (www.a2a.org.uk or www.nationalarchives.gov.uk/a2a), which lists an increasing proportion of holdings of local record offices and some more specialist archives.

The most important national repositories and museums are described in Appendix I. Regimental and service museums are described in Terence and Shirley Wise, *A Guide to Military Museums and Other Places of Military Interest* (10th edition, Terence Wise, 2001) or online (regimental museums only) at www.armymuseums.org.uk.

Every county has a local record office and most towns have a local studies or history centre. Yellow Pages or the local library should be able to tell you where it is located. Their holdings are described in Janet Foster and Julia Sheppard, *British Archives: a Guide to Archive Resources in the United Kingdom* (3rd edition, Palgrave, 2001), along with the vast majority of specialist repositories – every reference library should have a copy. Less comprehensive, but more practical, is Jeremy Gibson and Pamela Peskett, *Record Offices and How to Find Them* (8th edition, Federation of Family History Societies, 2002).

The ARCHON section of The National Archives website (www.archon.nationalarchives.gov.uk) provides links to most local record offices. It can be much harder, however, to track down local studies libraries, particularly ones outside your area. You can find many addresses through the Familia website (www.familia.org.uk), otherwise see whether your local library has a copy of the *Library Directory 1991-1992* which contains details of local studies libraries and their holdings.

FINDING WHAT YOU WANT

Each record office has a different system of managing its records, although most follow the same principles of archive administration. Documents are kept together by collection, rather than rearranged by subject as happens in a library. This can be frustrating if you are researching a topic, as you may have to search a number of sources to find what you want. A number of repositories have electronic catalogues, notably at The National Archives, which identify documents in a large number of places on the same subject (www.catalogue.nationalarchives.gov.uk). They are also usually available online. The online Access to Archives (A2A) catalogue (www.a2a.org.uk) provides the same service for local record offices and some military museums. A2A is extremely easy to use, although it is by no means comprehensive. However, you are unlikely to be able to track down an individual, as the catalogues only record the item description, rather than describe the contents, so you may well have to look through records from a particular regiment or battalion before you turn up a reference to your ancestor.

The majority of records described in this book are to be found at The National Archives (TNA) at Kew. TNA records are arranged by lettercode – you are most likely to use records created by the War Office (prefix WO), Admiralty (ADM) or Air Ministry (AIR). The types of records are arranged by series (sometimes called classes), so RAF Squadron Operation Record Books (ORB) are in series AIR 27, while ORBs for RAF stations are in AIR 28. Within the series each file or volume has been assigned a separate file number. The ORB for RAF Tangmere between June 1925 and December 1944 is in piece AIR 28/815. To an extent, with the arrival of the electronic catalogue, this no longer matters, but occasionally it can be still useful to know how the records are organised.

Many local record offices, local studies libraries and some regimental museums, however, still rely on old-fashioned card indexes arranged by subjects. There's usually a heading for the 'Second World War' or perhaps others for 'memorials' or 'conscription'.

UNDERTAKING RESEARCH

It is important to ring beforehand to book a seat as most archives have very cramped reading areas. They should also be able to give you a rough idea whether they have the records you are interested in, and indeed may have something ready when you arrive. They can also tell you whether they allow the use of laptop computers, digital cameras and other gadgets.

You should take with you a notebook, several pencils (as pens are rarely allowed into reading rooms), any notes you might have, a pound coin for a locker for your bag and coat (should they be provided). It is a good idea to allow plenty of time to familiarise yourself with the archive and its finding aids, particularly if you are going to make several visits. You may also want to talk through what you hope to find with the archivist or librarian on duty, as they may be able to suggest places to look and shortcuts to take.

Many archives now allow you to take a digital camera to take shots of pages from documents, photographs and maps. This can save both time in making notes, and cost in ordering photocopies. As each archive has its own rules, it's a good idea to ask before taking your camera along.

Written sources are the basis of all historical research. Using them properly makes the best use of your time and ensures that you get all you can from the records. The best practice is to do the following:

- Note down all the references of the documents you consult, together with their descriptions, even for those items which were useless. You may need to use them again; having the references can cut the work in half.
- Read each document thoroughly, especially if you are unfamiliar with the type of record. See whether there is an index at the front or back which could help.
- Many records come in similar form. Operation Record Books or battalion war diaries, for example, are much the same. Once you have mastered the style they are easy to go through.
- There may be an index or other finding aid. Ask the staff.
- If you are not sure about how to use a document or reading it, ask the staff. They are there to help!
- Note down everything of interest together with the reference of the document in a notebook, in case you need to look at the item again on a future visit. Try to keep your notes legible (not, of course, a problem if you are using a laptop computer).

MAKING USE OF YOUR RESEARCH

Although research is a deeply satisfying pastime in itself, you should aim to write up your study and publish it in some way, so that other people can make use of your work (think how you benefited from the research of others) and admire your perspicacity! There are three main ways of doing this:

- You may be able to persuade a local or military history society to publish your work, alternatively you can either publish the book yourself or approach a publisher to do it for you. Whatever you do, you are unlikely to make a profit.
- Submit an article to a family, local or military history journal (depending on the subject). Editors usually welcome well-written, interesting contributions. Don't make it too long: two or three thousand words maximum. *The Second World War* is a new magazine devoted to the war which is looking for material. Details are given in Appendix II.
- Putting your research on the internet is an increasingly popular alternative. It is almost free and there is literally a worldwide audience waiting to read what you've written, although it is not as easy to create an attractive site that people will want to come back to as it might seem at first glance. Most internet service providers (ISPs) will display your web pages for free. It is surprisingly easy to do – even for technical novices, as there are a number of books and magazines, and even internet sites, which can help you.

2

COMMON SOURCES

This chapter describes the records which were common to all services. It's a good idea to read this before turning to the following individual chapters.

SERVICE RECORDS

Unlike the First World War when almost half the men serving in the forces were volunteers, almost all servicemen in the Second World War were conscripts. In the years before the outbreak of war various schemes were prepared to ensure adequate manpower in case of war. In May 1939 the Military Training Act came into effect. This meant that all men on reaching the age of 20 were required to join the Army, Royal Navy or Royal Air Force. They were allowed to choose which branch of service to enter.

On the outbreak of war, the National Service Act came into effect on 6 September 1939. This called for conscription of all males between the ages of 18 and 41, who again could choose which service to join, although this choice was not always granted. A second act was passed in December 1941 which extended conscription to women, and raised the upper age limit for men to 51. As well as the services, men could now be assigned to the Auxiliary Fire Service, the Police War Reserve, or industry, and from late 1943 could be sent down the mines (see Chapter 7 below). Men and women from Northern Ireland were exempt from conscription.

Service records, for both officers and other ranks who served in the forces after 1920, are still held by the Ministry of Defence. Veterans and next of kin can request copies for which a charge, currently £30, is made (although this may be waived for veterans themselves and their widows). More details are given at: www.veteransagency.mod.uk. Each service maintains its own record office, each of which are very busy so you may have to wait a few months before your request is dealt with:

- *Army:* Army Personnel Centre Historical Disclosures, Mail Point 400, Kentigern House, 65 Brown Street, Glasgow G2 8EX. A few regiments still keep their own records. Their details are given in Chapter 3.
- *Royal Navy and Merchant Navy:* All Royal Naval personnel were given their service record when they were discharged. For pension purposes the Navy retained pay details. Therefore the only information held for seamen and officers is their service details (number, rank, name, etc) and a list of dates and ships/shore bases. Write to: DPS(N)2, Building 1/152 , PP65 Victory View, HMNB Portsmouth PO1 3LS.

  Each rating's service number had a combination of letters before it signifying the branch he was with and designated port. The abbreviations for branches were: J (Seamen), K (Stokers), L (Stewards and Cooks), M (Miscellaneous); and for ports: C (Chatham), D (Devonport), F (Fleet Air Arm) and P (Portsmouth). In addition the letter X meant that the individual adhered to the new pay code introduced in 1925, and an S meant special service engagement (that is, for the duration of the war). Service records for Merchant seamen and officers are described in Chapter 5.
- *Royal Air Force:* PMA IM 1B RAF, Room 5 Building 248A, RAF Personnel Management Agency, RAF Innsworth, Gloucester GL3 1EZ.

OFFICERS

Details of all officers are given in directories, known as lists, which were published several times a year. The National Archives has complete sets of *The Army List, The Navy List* and *The Air Force List* for the Second World War period on open shelves in the Microfilm Reading Room, and you should find sets at other military museums and archives. Although there are some differences between them, essentially they indicate the unit to which an officer was attached, promotions, and whether they had attended a staff college. They are authoritative, so if a man does not appear in their pages then he was not an officer.

FINDING OLD COMRADES

If you are trying to find a comrade who served with your father or grandmother or want to know more about what a particular unit got up to, there may still be somebody who can remember. Of course those who served are now getting old, so they need to be treated with courtesy and respect.

There are many ways to track down veterans. One of the best is through the Royal British Legion, whose *Legion* magazine includes a 'lost trails' page. Details are given in Appendix I. Provided you know the unit your relative served with, regimental associations may be willing to put appeals in their magazines and newsletters. For the RAF, write to the Royal Air Forces Association, Central Headquarters, 43 Grove Park Road, London W4 3RU to insert an appeal in their *Airmail Magazine*. There are also several websites, such as www.servicepals.com and www.forcesreunited.org.uk, which offer the same service. Lists of RAF associations and links to their websites can be found at www.associations.rafinfo.org.uk.

MEDALS AND AWARDS

CAMPAIGN MEDALS

Every serviceman and woman who met certain criteria (normally being present for 90 days in a particular theatre of operations) could claim up to five campaign medals. As a general rule, most service personnel were not issued with medals before they were demobilised. Consequently they had to claim them after they had left the services. Only those men and women who remained in the Armed Forces received their medals automatically. Although the availability of medals for wartime service was widely advertised at the time, many people did not claim them. Even now over 60 years later, several hundred veterans or their next of kin make an initial claim for Second World War medals every month. They are still issued, in the first instance, free of charge. Medals can be issued to the legal next of kin of deceased service personnel, but proof of kinship is required.

To claim medals, replace stolen or destroyed medals, or find out whether an individual is entitled please write to the MoD Medal Office (address below). You will need to supply service number, unit (Army and Marines) and branch or trade (RAF and RN), full name, date of birth, rank and date of discharge. As large numbers of people are claiming their medals, there is usually a backlog. Claims are dealt with as quickly as possible. Every effort is made to acknowledge and process claims in a timely manner, but checking and verification is a time-consuming process. For more information visit www.veteransagency.mod.uk. It is expected that over time the appropriate medal rolls and records will be transferred to The National Archives, but probably not for ten to fifteen years or so.

There is a medals office for the three services: MOD Medal Office, Building 250, RAF Innsworth, Gloucester GL3 1HW; tel: 01452 712612 ext 8149; www.veteransagency.mod.uk/medals_folder/medals_campaign_medals.htm.

Eight separate campaign medals were issued, although no more than five could be worn by an individual. As a cost-saving measure medals were not inscribed with the names of the individuals to whom they were awarded, although a number of people subsequently had inscriptions added privately. The campaign stars awarded to service personnel look identical from a distance. Only the distinctive ribbons and the wording on the medal itself indicate in which theatres of operations an individual fought. British medals were made in copper-zinc alloy, although the equivalents issued by Commonwealth countries were in silver.

The medals were:

1939-1945 Star — Three equal stripes of dark blue, scarlet and light blue, representing the three armed services. This was the basic war service star and was generally awarded to men who had completed six months' active service (two months for aircrew) overseas. It was the only medal awarded to men who saw service in France and Norway in 1940 and Greece and Crete in 1941. Those awarded this star were eligible for others if they served in other theatres of operation.

Air Crew Europe Star — A broad central light blue stripe, black borders and narrow yellow stripes, for the sky, the night

Left to right: The 1939-45 Star; The Defence Medal; and the Africa Star.

	and searchlight beams. Awarded to RAF crews for operational flights over Europe.
Atlantic Star	Three shaded equal stripes of dark blue, white and green. Generally awarded to those in the Royal and Merchant Navy who served in convoys across the North Atlantic, but members of the RAF and Army attached to the RN and Merchant Navy also received it.
Africa Star	Pale buff with a broad central scarlet stripe and two narrow stripes of dark blue (to the left) and mid blue (to the right). Awarded for one or more days' service anywhere in North Africa before 12 May 1943.
Burma Star	A central red stripe and two narrower blue and yellow stripes on either side. Awarded for service in India and Burma.
Italy Star	Equal stripes of red, white, green, white and red representing the Italian flag. Awarded for service in Italy, the Balkans and southern France between 11 June 1943 and 8 May 1945.
Pacific Star	Dark green with scarlet edges, a central yellow stripe, a narrow dark blue stripe on the left side

	and a light blue one on the right. Also awarded to personnel who served in Hong Kong and Malaya.
Defence Medal	Green (for the fields of Britain), with a wide central orange stripe (the flames of the Blitz) and two narrower black stripes either side (for those who lost their lives during the bombing). Awarded to all those who served in a military capacity in Britain, Malta and the British colonies between September 1939 and May 1945, including civilians and members of the Home Guard.
War Service Medal	The colours of the Union Flag going from red to blue to white from each edge and a narrow central red stripe. Issued to anyone who served 28 days in uniform or in an accredited organisation.

More about these medals can be found in an article by John Sly in *Ancestors Magazine* (July 2005). They are also described in more detail in Peter Duckers, *British Campaign Medals 1914-2000* (Shire Publications, 2002), Robert W. Gould, *British Campaign Medals: Waterloo to the Gulf* (Arms and Armour Press, 1994) and L.L. Gordon (et al), *British Battles and Medals* (Spink & Son Ltd, 1988).

GALLANTRY MEDALS

Gallantry medals were awarded for acts of heroism and bravery on the field of battle. Details of all awards were published (sometimes referred to as 'gazetted') in the *London Gazette*, occasionally with a citation (that is, a description of how the medal was won), although in most cases it is not possible to find out very much about why a medal was awarded. At the very least you will get the man's name, service number, rank, regiment and the date when the award was made. The National Archives has copies (in series ZJ 1), together with indexes in the Microfilm Reading Room. The *Gazette* may also be found in other libraries and is available online (fully indexed) at www.gazettes-online.co.uk. The award of gallantry medals to individuals may sometimes be mentioned in war diaries or operation record books.

Some 181 awards for the Victoria Cross were made during the war. There are several websites devoted to the VC, of which www.chapter-one.com/vc is the most comprehensive, with detailed biographies of all VC winners. A register of those holding the VC can be found in piece WO 98/8 at TNA, together with copies of citations and other information. It is also available online at www.nationalarchives.gov.uk/documentsonline. Another list is in CAB 106/312.

Simple descriptions and illustrations of all gallantry medals, regardless of service, can be found in Peter Duckers, *British Gallantry Medals 1914-2000* (Shire Publications, 2002) and P.E. Abbott and J.M.A. Tamplin, *British Gallantry Awards* (Nimrod Dix, 1981). See also the sections on medals in Chapter 3 (Army), Chapter 4 (Royal Navy), Chapter 5 (Merchant Marine) or Chapter 6 (Royal Air Force) below.

CASUALTIES

The dead of the Second World War are recorded in many ways, all of which can provide useful information about an ancestor who sacrificed their life for the greater good. Death certificates for these men and women can be found in the normal way at the Family Records Centre. For more about this see the entry under the Centre in Appendix I.

COMMONWEALTH WAR GRAVES COMMISSION

The Commonwealth War Graves Commission was set up to commemorate the dead of the First World War and has done its best to find and record as many war deaths of British and Commonwealth men and women as possible. It is perhaps best known for the hundreds of carefully tended, and very moving, cemeteries scattered across the world. Their database, also known as the Debt of Honour Roll, is online at www.cwgc.org and this will tell you where a man is buried, when he died, his rank and the unit he served with. It also includes civilian deaths of the Second World War. A recent feature is a history of individual cemeteries, which can prove to be surprisingly informative, and you can often download plot layouts so you can easily find where a man is buried. You can also write to or telephone the Commission for information about an individual: Commonwealth

The El Alamein cemetery in Egypt with the Cross of Sacrifice found in every Commonwealth War Graves Commission cemetery in the background. (Courtesy: Mike Booker)

War Graves Commission, 2 Marlow Road, Maidenhead SL6 7DX; tel: 01628-34221; www.cwgc.org.

WAR MEMORIALS

Unlike after the First World War, relatively few new war memorials were erected to the dead (although there has been a spate in recent years). Instead, names of the fallen were generally added to existing memorials. They take a variety of forms – the most common is a memorial cross, but they vary from playing fields to hospital buildings. An ancestor may appear on two or three such memorials, or in rare cases may have been missed off altogether. Normally all you will find is his name,

The gravestone for Private Adam Wakenshaw, Durham Light Infantry, in the Alamein Cemetery. He won the Victoria Cross in June 1942 for protecting his company while they withdrew, despite being mortally wounded. (Courtesy: Mike Booker)

sometimes the rank and unit, and details of gallantry medals will also be included. In small villages everybody who served in the forces may be included, not just the deceased.

The UK National Inventory of War Memorials, based at the Imperial War Museum, is identifying and preparing a database of memorials for all wars. The database can be consulted online at www.ukiwm.org.uk. Their records sometimes include transcriptions of what is written on the memorials, but this is by no means universal, although they have just started a project to collect the names of people.

A number of studies about the men or women whose names appear on local war memorials have been carried out in recent years, although researchers have generally concentrated on the fallen of the First World War. Even so it is worth asking in your local library to see whether one has been done for your area.

HOSPITAL RECORDS

Few, if any, records for individuals, either wounded or sick, survive. However, if the hospital to which your ancestor was admitted for treatment was in Britain (and you know which one) it might be worth checking the Wellcome Institute/National Archives database of hospital records (www.nationalarchives.gov.uk/hospitalrecords) to see whether any patient records survive.

If you know at which hospitals or casualty clearing stations your ancestor was a patient, you may find reports in the records of the official historian of the medical services for the Army in series WO 222 and for the Navy in ADM 261 at Kew. The equivalent for the RAF is in AIR 49, and includes reports, correspondence and other papers from various commands, groups, wings, squadrons and maintenance units stationed in many parts of the world; and from Hospital, Mobile Field Hospitals and Medical Receiving Stations and other units, including a few from the Commonwealth. There is material, including consultants' reports, in a number of medical fields, and on the condition, reception and care of prisoners of war. It is unlikely, however, that you will find very much about individuals.

The Joint War Organisation of the British Red Cross and Order of St John also ran a number of auxiliary hospitals in the UK. They are listed in P.G. Cambray and G.G.B. Briggs, *Red Cross and St John: the Official Record of the Humanitarian Services of the War Organisation of the British Red Cross Society and Order of St John of Jerusalem* (London, 1949), with a brief history at www.redcross.org.uk/standard.asp?id=39704. Unfortunately, no patients' records survive from any of these institutions.

PRISONERS OF WAR

There are extensive collections of records at The National Archives (TNA) which are described in a TNA Research Guide *British Prisoners of War 1939-1953*. The Imperial War Museum also has many documents including memoirs from former PoWs and camp newspapers.

LISTS OF PRISONERS

The most comprehensive nominal listings of British and

Commonwealth PoWs at The National Archives are found in pieces WO 392/1-26. They include prisoners from each of the services and the merchant navy held in Germany or German-occupied territory; prisoners of all services and the merchant navy held in Italy; and service personnel (not merchant navy) and some civilian internees held by the Japanese either in Japan or Japanese-occupied territory in September 1944. These lists are in roughly alphabetical order by theatre of operations and can be downloaded for a fee (at time of writing – £3.50) from TNA's Documents Online service at www.nationalarchives.gov.uk/documentsonline.

In 1990 the Imperial War Museum reprinted ten volumes of *Germany and German Occupied Territories: Imperial Prisoners of War: Alphabetical Lists* (His Majesty's Stationery Office, 1945), which listed approximately 169,000 British and Commonwealth prisoners of all ranks held in Germany and German-occupied territories, with details of name, rank and service/army number as well as regiment/corps, prisoner of war number and, presumably, their final camp location details: *Prisoners of War: British Army 1939-1945* (J.B. Hayward & Son, 1990) and *Prisoners of War: Naval and Air Forces of Great Britain and the Empire, 1939-1945* (J.B. Hayward & Son, 1990).

In the Research Enquiries Room at Kew there is a typescript research guide, *British Prisoners of War, World War Two*, which includes full document references, dates and descriptions for: reports on camps; nominal lists; escape and evasion reports; and miscellaneous reports. However, although still useful, this guide has been largely superseded by entries in the online catalogue.

FAR EAST

Prisoners of the Japanese are listed on index cards in WO 345 at Kew; some 56,000 pre-printed cards of uncertain provenance that appear to have been compiled by a central Japanese authority. The cards, with certain exceptions, record in Japanese and/or English: camp; name; nationality; rank; place of capture; father's name; place of origin; date of birth; unit and service number; date of capture; mother's name; occupation; remarks. Other information is found on the reverse and may include medical details etc. A diagonal red line across the card appears to indicate that the prisoner is dead.

Three registers in WO 367 record the names of some 13,500 Allied prisoners of war and civilian internees of British and other nationalities held in camps in Singapore. The registers give minimal information about each prisoner and were apparently compiled for the Japanese camp administration, although the majority of the information is in English. The registers refer to camps numbered 1-4 but the identity of these has not been established.

A website devoted to the experiences of Allied prisoners in the Far East can be found at www.cofepow.org.uk.

LIBERATION QUESTIONNAIRES

TNA has approximately 140,000 Liberation Questionnaires (found in series WO 344) completed by mainly British and Commonwealth PoWs of all ranks and services, plus a few other Allied nationals and merchant seamen. While the plans to question all liberated PoWs never materialised, these records nevertheless represent a large percentage, perhaps as high as 90 per cent, of those still in captivity in 1945. They are arranged alphabetically by name sequences with separate sections for those held by Germany and Japan.

As well as giving personal details, name, rank, number, unit and home address, these records can include: date and place of capture; main camps and hospitals in which imprisoned and work camps; serious illnesses suffered while a prisoner and medical treatment received; interrogation after capture; escape attempts; sabotage; suspicion of collaboration by other Allied prisoners; details of bad treatment by the enemy to themselves or others. In addition, individuals were given the opportunity to bring to official notice any other matters, such as courageous acts by fellow prisoners or details of civilians who assisted them during escape and evasion activities. Consequently, additional documentation is sometimes attached.

ESCAPE REPORTS

Prisoners of war were expected to try to escape and many attempts were made, a few of which were successful. Escape reports, completed by those men who made it back to Britain from the Continent, are in three series: WO 208/3298-3327, 4238-4276, 4368-4371. Every report has a narrative, of variable length, which describes an individual's experiences as an escaper, evader or prisoner of war. In addition, many include appendices which, if they survive, can provide the names and addresses of civilian helpers, nature of help given, and relevant dates; details of the escape method and Allied personnel who assisted in an escape; details of the usefulness of officially provided escape aids, which ones were used, and suggested improvements and/or additions that could be made. There is a card index to the first series of reports in the Research Enquiries Room at Kew. The others are arranged by surname of escaper.

INTERNATIONAL RESOURCES

The International Committee of the Red Cross in Geneva keeps incomplete lists of all known PoWs and internees for the Second World War. Searches are only made in response to written enquiries, and an hourly fee is charged. The address is International Council of the Red Cross, Archives Division, 19 Avenue de la Paix, CH-1202 Geneva. More information can be found at www.icrc.org and www.redcross.org.uk/standard.asp?id=2627. There might also be information in American records (see Chapter 9 below). A fascinating website devoted to Allied servicemen who escaped through Belgium and the brave Belgians who helped them is at www.belgiumww2.info.

OTHER SOURCES

PERSONAL PAPERS

If you are lucky, one of the most interesting sources you may come across in the course of your research will be personal papers. They may take many forms: diaries, memoirs, photographs or ephemera, such as service discharge papers or looted German weaponry. These may still be in the possession of the veteran or their families or they may have been deposited with a museum or archive. If you have any such papers you should consider giving them (or at least supplying copies) to an archive repository for safekeeping and so that other people can use the material in their own researches.

There is no national collection of such material and it can be difficult to track down items for specific units or operations. However, there are two online databases which may supply clues: Access to Archives (www.nationalarchives.gov.uk/a2a or www.a2a.org.uk) and the National Register of Archives (www.nra.nationalarchives.org.uk).

The largest collection of personal papers and artefacts is held by the Imperial War Museum (IWM) in London. There are also collections of the papers of senior defence personnel at the Liddle Hart Archive in London, the Churchill Archive Centre in Cambridge, the National Maritime Museum and at the IWM itself, and there is an index to many of these papers at www.kcl.ac.uk/lhcma. Addresses are given in Appendix I below.

Regimental, naval and aviation museums collect papers of men who served with the regiment or other unit or otherwise have a close link to it. Local museums and record offices may also have papers, perhaps for men who were members of the Home Guard or employed in war work locally.

NEWSPAPERS AND MAGAZINES

Although newspapers were heavily censored, and much thinner than their pre-war equivalents because of paper rationing, they are still useful resources. Local newspapers may contain short biographies of men who won gallantry medals, had been posted as prisoners of war, or were killed in action. In the case of gallantry medals, stories are likely to appear at about the time the medal was gazetted. Biographies of the deceased would appear after the news was publicly announced, which might be some time after the actual death. Even if you can't find your ancestor in their pages, newspapers give a flavour of life on the home front, such as rationing, bombing raids and prosecutions for engaging in black market activities.

Local newspapers are generally available at county libraries and record offices, usually on microfilm. If they haven't got what you want you may have to go the British Library Newspaper Library at Colindale in North London, which has a complete set of almost all British and many Commonwealth newspapers. For more details see Appendix I.

National papers provide details of the progress of the war in general both overseas and at home, but also often fill their pages with minor news items, such as the appearance of individuals in the courts (particularly in London) and strange occurrences. With the exception of *The Times* and *The Scotsman*, there are no indexes, so it can be difficult to find an individual or an event. *The Times* is now available online as *The Times Digital Archive* at larger libraries. You can also use it on the public terminals in TNA reading rooms. It is a superb resource allowing you to print out the actual news story as it appeared in the paper. There are also detailed published indexes in book form (referred to as Palmer's Index, after the newspaper's chief librarian who began indexing the paper) and on CD. *The Scotsman* is online at http://archive.scotsman.com. There is a free search, but you will have to register and pay a subscription fee to see any results.

The armed forces published a variety of newspapers and magazines – either for distribution to everyone in a particular theatre of operations or service, or produced by the men of a particular unit. The best known service newspapers were *Union Jack* and, for the Army, *The Soldier* which was first published in 1944 and is still going strong. As well as news of the war and the home front there are likely to be articles (often humorous) on life in the unit, cartoons and photographs. Unit newspapers or magazines can be very hard to track down, but both the BL Newspaper Library and the Imperial War Museum have extensive collections. A comprehensive list can be found in Michael Anglo, *Service Newspapers of the Second World War* (Jupiter, 1977). Details of service newspapers and magazines published by the three services and for overseas forces can be found at www.naval-history.net. Regimental or service museums may also have copies for their regiment or branch. See Appendix I for details.

PHOTOGRAPHS AND FILM

The largest collection of photographs and cinema film is to be found at the Imperial War Museum. At the heart of the Museum's collections are the official photographs taken by British and Commonwealth photographers, supplemented by material donated by former servicemen. The Museum's Photographic Archive cannot tell you whether they have any pictures of your ancestor. However, they welcome visitors to search the photographic collections although advance booking is necessary. It is possible to buy copies of any of the pictures you are interested in. A selection of images has been put online as part of the IWM's catalogue (www.iwmcollection.org.uk). The postal address for the IWM is in Appendix I. The Archive's reading room, however, is in the All Saints Annexe, Austral St, London SE11 – a few minutes walk from the Museum itself, phone 020 7416 5333.

Regimental museums are also likely to have collections of material. Another source is commercial picture libraries, many of which have online image banks, although you may have to pay if you want to buy a particular picture. The largest is Getty Image (www.creative.gettyimages.com).

The IWM also has an incomparable film collection. At its heart is the uncut record footage filmed by combat cameramen. There is an online database to some 23,000 films at www.iwmcollections.org.uk/ qryfilm.asp which can be searched by individual or place. Again, to use the Museum's Film and Video Archive, you will need to make an appointment. They can also copy material to VHS for you to view at home. Like the Photographic Archive, they are based in the All Saints Annexe. Their phone number is 020 7416 5291 and details of their services can also be found at http://collections.iwm.org.uk/server/ show/nav.00g004.

There are also a number of regional film archives which have films of the period (generally, but not always, about the Home Front). Details are given at www.flickernow.org/sections-article140-page1.htm. The largest of these is the North West Film and Video Archive in Manchester. For more about using film archives in family history see an article in issue 82 of *Family History Monthly*.

If you have a broadband connection, newsreels from the period can be downloaded (free) from www.britishpathe.com.

CENTRAL DIRECTION OF THE WAR

One of the great joys of researching the Second World War is that virtually all the records are now available, so it is possible to see how the great decisions were made and read the papers which were presented to the war leaders. I still remember the thrill of seeing for the first time a minute to the Prime Minister with a pithy note in Churchill's own handwriting demanding 'action this day'. To make the best use of these sources it helps to have done some background reading on the history of the war and certainly to know the codenames assigned to any specific operations you are researching. A list of common abbreviations and the most common codenames used is in Appendix III.

There are several series of records at The National Archives, most of which are well indexed, that can be consulted. They may also be available on microfilm in university libraries. More information can be found in a TNA research guide, *Second World War, 1939-1945: the War Cabinet*.

Formal decisions were taken by the War Cabinet: that is, the Prime Minister and a few senior ministers. Minutes are in series CAB 65 at Kew and memoranda presented for discussion or information in CAB 66. Unfortunately any sense of the drama and debates that must have taken place, particularly during June and July 1940, does not appear in the dry notes of the meetings. However, notebooks consisting of rough minutes taken by the Cabinet Secretary for cabinet meetings between 1943 and 1945 have recently been transferred into CAB 195 and give a flavour of the debates which took place. There were also a large number of Cabinet committees which looked at all aspects of the war and the post-war world, the most important of which was the Lord President's Committee, under the Deputy Prime Minister Clement Attlee, which effectively oversaw the war effort on the home front. As the war progressed decisions, particularly military ones, inevitably were taken elsewhere than the War Cabinet, generally by the Chiefs of Staff (minutes in CAB 79, memoranda in CAB 80) or the Anglo-American Combined Chiefs of Staff (papers in CAB 88).

Memoranda and related papers presented to the Prime Minister are in PREM 3 (or to Neville Chamberlain in PREM 1). Churchill made it a clear rule that 'all directions emanating from me are made in writing'. As a result, the series offers a complete record of the war from Churchill's perspective, including his directives, memoranda and general papers submitted to him for discussion. Examples of items featured include Lord Trenchard's views on Air Policy, Mountbatten on General MacArthur, Churchill's telegrams to Stalin and other leaders, papers concerning defence plans for Singapore and Australia, records of Anglo-American discussions, papers on Japan, the Soviet Union, Overlord, Torch, Submarine Warfare, SOE and Occupied Europe. The equivalent for the home front is in PREM 4.

To get a flavour of what life must have been like for Churchill and his advisors it is well worth visiting the Cabinet War Rooms, where the Cabinet met many times during the war and where the Prime Minister and his staff lived during air raids. The complex also houses a museum dedicated to the life and work of Winston Churchill. Details are at http://cwr.iwm.org.uk.

More about the organisation and planning of operations can be found in the appropriate place in the Army, Navy and Air Force chapters below.

3

THE BRITISH ARMY

SERVICE RECORDS

Most records are held by the Army Personnel Centre in Glasgow, whose address is given in Chapter 2. However, the Household Cavalry and Guards regiments keep their own records:

- Household Cavalry Museum, Combermere Barracks, St Leonards Road, Windsor SL4 3DN; tel: 01753 755112; www.householdcavalry.gvon.com/museum.htm.
- Guards Museum, Wellington Barracks, Birdcage Walk, London SW1E 6HQ.

OFFICERS

All officers are named in the *Army Lists*, which were published quarterly during the war. For intelligence reasons the information given is not as comprehensive as would be found in peacetime lists. Even so it should be possible to track down promotions and the date they were made. There were in fact two series, the Half Yearly and Quarterly, but both contain similar information. The National Archives has a complete set on the shelves in the Microfilm Reading Room, and copies can be found elsewhere.

Biographical details of officers in the Army Medical Corps are listed in Sir William Macfarlane's *A List of Commissioned Medical Officers of the Army, 1660-1960* (Wellcome Library, 1968). Both The National Archives and Society of Genealogists' libraries have copies. A little bit more about researching medical personnel, including nurses, can be found at www.army-medical-history.co.uk.

MEDALS

Campaign and gallantry medals for Army personnel are largely the same as the other services and are described in Chapter 2 above. Most recommendations for the VC, DSO, MC, DCM and MM (and a very few Mentions in Despatches) are in series WO 373 (from 1938) at Kew. To find them you will need to know when the award appeared in the *London Gazette* and the theatre of war. The Distinguished Service Order (DSO) was normally only awarded to senior officers, while the Military Cross (MC) was awarded for acts of bravery to officers of the rank of captain or below. A register, arranged by the date the awards appeared in the *London Gazette*, is in WO 390/9-13. Extracts from the *London Gazette* for the award of the Military Cross can be found in WO 389. Even if your ancestor was not in the Army it may be worth checking as some members of the RN, the RAF, Royal Marines and the Home Guard received Army awards.

ARMY ROLL OF HONOUR

The creation of an Army Roll of Honour, now at The National Archives in series WO 304, was first discussed in the War Office in January 1944, as a direct result of the failure of accurate lists published in the national press. It was soon realised that a single roll of honour would enable the War Office, units of the British Army and other organisations to obtain data concerning casualties from a single source, and so be less time consuming than consulting a variety of other records.

The roll was compiled between the end of 1944 and March 1949 for the use of the War Office and the Commonwealth War Graves Commission. Information on the original roll is contained in both plain and coded text. Apart from surname and forenames, army service number and date of death, all other information (rank, first unit served in, unit serving in at time of death, place of birth, place of domicile and place of death), was given numerical codes. Individuals found in the roll died between 1 September 1939 and 31 December 1946, and also included are those deaths in service which were non-attributable (natural causes, etc) as well as those, of course, who were killed in action or who died of wounds or disease. The roll does not include 'disgraceful' deaths: for men executed for capital crimes while in the Army, for example. It is now available in a fully

Evacuating casualties of the 6th Battalion, Grenadier Guards at Monte Camino, November-December 1943. (From The Grenadier Guards 1939-1945, *Gale and Polden, 1946)*

searchable form on CD, at many libraries and archives, or you can buy a copy from Naval and Military Press (for details see Appendix II). The disc may also be called *Soldiers Died in the Second World War 1939-1945*. It is also online (for a fee) at www.military-genealogy.co.uk.

OPERATIONAL RECORDS

WAR DIARIES

While on active service, Army headquarters, formations and units were required to keep war diaries recording their daily activities. The purpose of the diaries was twofold: to provide data on which future improvements in training, equipment, organisation and administration could be based; and to provide future historians with a record of activities of units and formations in operational periods. They generally consist of war diary or intelligence summary sheets,

A familiar sight for many soldiers were the troopships, which were often converted liners. Conditions for the men were sometimes primitive, although officers fared rather better. (From Merchantmen at War: The Official Story of the Merchant Navy 1939-1944, *HMSO, 1944)*

Soldiers catch a few minutes' rest in the hours after D-Day. (Courtesy: Imperial War Museum)

located at the beginning, which record the date of each entry, the unit's location, a summary of events and any remarks or references to appendices. The appendices, which make up the larger part of each diary, may include: strength and casualty returns, routine orders and administrative instructions, operation orders and instructions, reports, messages, location statements, intelligence summaries, and occasionally photographs, sketches, maps and traces. They can be of particular interest to family historians as they may contain signals, unit orders and lists of men being transferred in or out of the unit.

The war diaries vary greatly in the amount and level of detailed information they contain. Their quality generally reflects the skill, dedication and enthusiasm of the officers in charge of compiling them. They are, however, a key record source and you will need to use them to build up a picture of your ancestor's Army service. It is uncommon for individuals, particularly ordinary soldiers, to be mentioned by name. The names of officers are usually given when they were wounded (or killed) or undertook an unusual operation. However, the lack of personal names is not necessarily important: knowing that your ancestor was in that unit is sufficient to build up a picture of what he was engaged in.

The war diaries are arranged by theatre of operations, so you need to know where your ancestor served. If you are not sure, you should consult the Orders of Battle (see below). The war diary references at TNA are:

WO 165 – War Office Directorates
WO 166 – Home Forces (forces stationed in the United Kingdom)
WO 167 – British Expeditionary Force (France 1939-1940)
WO 168 – North-West Expeditionary Force (Norway 1940)
WO 169 – Middle East Forces (Egypt and Libya, East Africa, Iraq, Iran)
WO 170 – Central Mediterranean Forces (Italy, Greece and Austria)
WO 171 – North-West Europe (France and Germany 1944-1945)
WO 172 – South-East Asia Command (India and Burma)
WO 173 – West Africa Forces
WO 174 – Madagascar
WO 175 – British North Africa Forces (Algeria and Tunisia 1942-1943)
WO 176 – Various smaller theatres (mainly Caribbean, Faeroes, Fiji, Gibraltar, Iceland)
WO 177 – Medical services
WO 178 – Military Missions
WO 179 – Dominion Forces
WO 215 – GHQ Liaison Regiment
WO 218 – Special Services

ORDERS OF BATTLE

Orders of battle (ORBAT) tell you which units were serving where and whose command they were under. They can be useful if you are trying to decide which series of war diaries to look at or work out relationships with higher echelons. There is a set in series WO 212. A number of websites also include ORBATs of varying degrees of accuracy and completeness. Probably the best, although strictly the information isn't taken from orders of battle, is to be found at www.regiments.org – the site is easy to use and arranged by regiment rather than by campaign or any other odd way devised by the webmaster. Other sites are http://home.adelphia.net/-dryan67/orders/army.html; http://homepages.force9.net/rothwell/index.htm and www.ordersofbattle.com. The best source in print is Lieutenant Colonel H.F. Joslen, *Orders of Battle: United Kingdom and Colonial and Dominion Formations in the Second World War* (HMSO, 1960, reprinted by Naval & Military Press, 2003).

PLANNING AND ANALYSIS

If you want to look at how your ancestor, or more likely his unit, fitted into the big picture then there are plenty of sources at The National Archives to help you. However, before you start, it is a good idea to read up on the campaign or battle you hope to research, as this provides the background which allows you to make something of the, at times, very complicated files. You might also want to look at Cabinet and related papers to see what Churchill and other political and military leaders thought about the operation or campaign. They are briefly described above.

The records of the military Headquarters of each theatre of operation, and of the forces under their command, are the most important sources of information on the planning and conduct of military operations. The most important series of records are for British Expeditionary Force in France 1939-1940 (WO 197); Home Forces (WO 199); Middle East Forces (WO 201); Far East Forces (WO 203); Italy and North Africa (WO 228); 21st Army Group in North West Europe (WO 205, WO 229); SHAEF (WO 219, WO 229), and Combined Operations (DEFE 2). Other useful sources are various series of files created by the War Office Directorate of Military Intelligence in WO 108, WO 190, WO 193 and WO 208. More about these records, and other sources, can be found in a TNA Research Guide, *Second World War: British Army Operations 1939-1945*.

OTHER SOURCES

COURTS MARTIAL

A court martial is a court convened to try an offence against military discipline, or against the ordinary law, committed by a person in one of the armed services. It was also used to try civilians when martial law was in force. Some records relating to individual cases of court martial are closed for 75 years from the last date on each file, which means that a few files relating to the Second World War are still not available. There were several types of court martial:

- General court martial (GCM): The Army's highest tribunal, dealing with commissioned officers and the most serious cases involving other ranks. It could only be convened by the Crown or its deputy (such as commanders-in-chief, governors general, etc).
- Field general court martial (FGCM): Often used in wartime. Only three commissioned officers needed to be present.
- District (or garrison) court martial (DCM): More limited in jurisdiction, these courts could not try commissioned officers or charges carrying prison sentences of more than two years. Details of the sentence were sent up to the Judge Advocate General's Office.
- Regimental court martial (RCM): Used for other ranks charged with lesser offences. Details may be noted in war diaries, but no records were sent to the Judge Advocate General's Office. Some of the records of these courts may survive among the records preserved by individual regiments at regimental museums.

Registers of courts martial at TNA are mainly in WO 213, with surviving case papers in WO 71 principally for the most important trials. There are some miscellaneous records in WO 93, including details of death penalties carried out after 1941 for murder and other capital crimes. More information is given in a TNA research guide, *British Army: Courts Martial, 17th-20th Centuries*.

MAPS

Maps were (and are) an essential part of military planning. Hundreds of thousands of maps were drawn and distributed during the war, few of which now survive. The major series of maps at TNA is to be found in WO 252, along with reports about strategic targets. Otherwise maps may be found in war diaries or in intelligence or other files. There is a card index to maps in the Map and Large Document Reading Room at Kew.

The British Library's Map Library also has good holdings of military maps, which include maps issued to troops involved in the Normandy landings on D-Day, silk maps which pilots carried concealed in their clothing in case they were shot down, and the invasion packs for most European countries prepared by the Germans and subsequently captured by the Allies. For details see Appendix I or visit: www.bl.uk/collections/map_modern_foreign.html. Regimental museums often have small collections.

SCOTLAND

As Scottish highland and lowland regiments, and the men who served in them, were part of the British Army their records are exactly the same as their English equivalents. There are, however, a few purely Scottish sources, which may be of interest. Deaths of Scottish soldiers, together with their marriages and baptisms of their children are with the General Register of Scotland, New Register House, Edinburgh EH1 3YT (www.gro-scotland.gov.uk). These records will shortly be made available online at www.scotlandspeople.gov.uk.

The National War Museum of Scotland has a number of collections relating to Scotland's military involvement in the Second World War, including a comprehensive library open to the public. No appointment is necessary but it is prudent to phone ahead. It is to be found in Edinburgh Castle, Edinburgh EH1 2NG; tel: 0131 225 7534; www.nms.ac.uk/war/index.htm.

Scotland's war dead, including 50,000 from the Second World War, are honoured at the Scots National War Memorial, again situated in the precincts of Edinburgh Castle. More information, together with a searchable database to names on the memorial, can be found at www.snwm.org.

The Scots at War Trust exists to encourage research into Scottish military history. They have an informative website at www.fettes.com/scotsatwar.

AUXILIARY TERRITORIAL SERVICE

The Women's Auxiliary Territorial Service was officially launched on 9 September 1938. The first women recruited worked as cooks, clerks and storekeepers. One interesting point was that women aged between 17 and 43 were allowed to join the service, although ATS

ASK FOR INFORMATION AT THE NEAREST EMPLOYMENT EXCHANGE OR AT ANY ARMY OR ATS. RECRUITING CENTRE

A recruiting poster for the Women's Auxiliary Territorial Service (ATS).

pay was only two thirds of the male rate. After the outbreak of the war, 300 members of the ATS were sent to France. ATS telephonists were some of the last people to leave the country during the retreat from Dunkirk. Conscription was introduced in 1941 and the girls of the ATS were then on an equal footing with the men and subject to military law. After 1941 many ATS girls served overseas. Peak strength of the ATS was reached in mid 1943 with 210,308 women in uniform. Their range of duties also expanded and women now served as office, mess and telephone orderlies, drivers, postal workers and ammunition inspectors. The ATS was regarded as being the least prestigious of the three service women's organisations until Princess Elizabeth (now the Queen) joined it in 1944. The service was absorbed into the new Women's Royal Army Corps in 1949.

Service records are with the Ministry of Defence (see Chapter 2). Few records about the ATS are to be found at The National Archives, but there may well be material at the Imperial War Museum, National Army Museum and Wellcome Library (addresses are given in Appendix I). Their story is told in Roy Terry, *Women in Khaki: the Story of the British Woman Soldier* (London: Columbus Books, 1988). An interesting website devoted to the ATS is: http://hometown.aol.co.uk/asummerof44/myhomepage/collection.html.

FIRST AID NURSING YEOMANRY

The courage of the FANYs during the Second World War is well told in Sebastian Faulk's novel *Charlotte Gray*. Very little is known about this remarkable voluntary corps. It was founded in 1907 by an eccentric, who envisaged a group of nurses on horseback riding over the battlefield to tend the wounded. During the Second World War, members undertook a wide range of roles throughout the world: 1,500 of them became wireless operators and coders within the Special Operations Executive and a few were dropped into occupied Europe. Twelve members died in concentration camps and three were awarded the George Cross. They were renamed the Princess Royal's Volunteer Corps in 1999.

Records relating to former members of the Yeomanry are at their headquarters: FANY (PRVC), TA Centre, 95 Horseferry Road, London SW1P 2DY. More information can be found at www.fany.org.uk. A charge may be made for searches in the records. Their history is told in Hugh Popham, *The FANY in*

Peace and War: The Story of the First Aid Nursing Yeomanry 1907-2003 (Pen & Sword, 2003). There are several sites devoted to them or their work in SOE including www.64-baker-street.org and www.spartacus.schoolnet.co.uk/FWWfany.htm.

NURSING SERVICES

Soldiers were nursed by members of Queen Alexandra's Imperial Military Nursing Service (QAIMNS), which was renamed Queen Alexandra's Royal Army Nursing Corps in 1950. More about their work can be found in Juliet Piggott, *Queen Alexandra's Royal Army Nursing Corps* (London: Leo Cooper, 1990) and in a TNA Research Guide, *British Army: Nurses and Nursing Services*. Service records are with the Ministry of Defence (see Chapter 2).

The Army Medical Services Museum, Keogh Barracks, Ash Vale, Aldershot GU12 5RQ (tel: 01252 868612) has records relating to the service and the women who served with it. Few records are to be found at The National Archives, but there may well be material at the Imperial War Museum, National Army Museum and Wellcome Library (addresses are given in Appendix I).

Nursing assistance was also provided by VADs (literally, Voluntary Aid Detachment) of the Red Cross and the Order of St John through their Joint War Organisation. They were sometimes called the Civil Nursing Reserve. The Organisation administered auxiliary hospitals and convalescent homes in Britain and much of the VAD service was performed here and consisted of general nursing duties. Many VADs also served in military hospitals. In addition, they carried out clerical and kitchen duties and, as many men were engaged in military service, they also took on roles such as ambulance drivers, civil defence workers and welfare officers, and some were sent overseas to help nurse servicemen there. Service cards for VADs are held by British Red Cross Museum and Archives, 44 Moorfields, London EC2Y 9AL. More details can be found at www.redcross.org.uk/standard.asp?id=3423.

HOME GUARD

On 14 May 1940, the Government broadcast a message asking for volunteers for the LDV (Local Defence Volunteers). The name was changed to the more homely Home Guard on 23 August 1940;

THE L.D.V. ARMLET (1940)

Newly enlisted members of the Local Defence Volunteers (later the Home Guard) parade in June 1940. (From John Radnor, It All Happened Before: The Home Guard through the Centuries, *Harrap, 1945)*

'Dad's Army' was the name retrospectively bestowed on the force by the long-running BBC comedy series in the late 1960s. The government expected 150,000 men to volunteer. Within the first month, 750,000 men had enlisted, and by the end of June 1940, the total number of volunteers was over one million. Most men who could fight were already in the forces and those that were left were either too young or too old for active service, or in reserved occupations. Members of the Home Guard were expected to fight an invasion of crack German troops with nothing more, initially, than a collection of old shotguns and pieces of gas pipe with bayonets welded on the end. The number of men in the Home Guard did not fall below one million until they were stood down on 4 December 1944 and finally disbanded on 31 December 1945.

Distributed amongst the Home Guard were special and very secretive Auxiliary Units, who were to become the nucleus of a British resistance movement should the Germans have successfully invaded. The exploits of one such unit is told in Donald Brown, *Somerset v Hitler: Secret Operations in the Mendips 1939-1945* (Countryside Books, 1999). The British Resistance Museum at Parham, Suffolk is dedicated to the AUs. Details can be found at www.parhamairfieldmuseum.co.uk/brohome.html.

Service records are held by the Ministry of Defence (see Chapter 2). Members were entitled to the Defence Medal after three years' service. In common with other wartime campaign medals it had to be applied for. For more details see Chapter 2.

Muster rolls for Home Guard units can sometimes be found at local record offices; for example, the Guildhall Library has rolls for units in the City of London and Essex. War diaries are in series WO 166 at Kew. A set of Home Guard lists, with details of officers and other information is available on the open shelves in the Microfilm Reading Room. More information about TNA sources are given in a TNA Research Guide, *Home Front: Second World War, 1939-1945*. Their story is told in S.P. MacKenzie, *The Home Guard: A Military and Political History* (Oxford University Press, 1995). A comprehensive website devoted to the Home Guard is www.home-guard.org.uk.

4

THE ROYAL NAVY

SERVICE RECORDS

Service details of men who served with the Royal Navy and Royal Marines are still held by the Ministry of Defence. They are described in Chapter 2.

OFFICERS

Details of officers are given in the *Navy Lists*, which are on the open shelves at The National Archives at Kew or available at museums such as the Royal Naval Museum in Portsmouth and the National Maritime Museum at Greenwich. In addition there is a series of *Confidential Navy Lists* which indicates where individual officers were serving, with the names of ships and establishments. A complete list of all ships in the Royal Navy is included, together with details of tonnage and armament. These can be found in series ADM 177 at Kew, with copies at major naval museums.

Series ADM 340 contains files and record-of-service cards, detailing the service of officers in the Royal Navy, the Royal Naval Reserve, the Royal Naval Volunteer Reserve and the Women's Royal Naval Service (WRNS), arranged in alphabetical order. Cards and files were introduced early in the 20th century for all officers then serving. These documents form a single continuous record spanning the length of the officer's service. Some records in this series therefore detail service through the war and into the 1950s.

Some summaries of confidential reports on captains and their

An officer on board a minelaying vessel. (From Ernest Fairfax, Calling All Arms: the Story of How a Loyal Company of British Men and Women Lived Through Six Historic Years, *Hutchinson, 1945)*

suitability for promotion up until 1943 are in series ADM 196/93-94. Photographs are attached to reports. Records for honorary officers who served in the RNR are in ADM 240.

RATINGS

Service records for men who served in the Royal Naval Reserve (RNR) are on microfilm in piece BT 377/77 at Kew. The records are arranged in service number order, although there are indexes if you do not have his number. The original records are with the Fleet Air Arm Museum (see Appendix I for the address).

MISCELLANEOUS SOURCES

The National Archives has a number of registers for baptisms, marriages and burials at naval chapels including those at Chatham and Shotley (ADM 338), Greenwich Royal Naval Hospital (ADM 73), and Sheerness (ADM 6). Registers of pharmacists who served in the Royal Navy can be found in piece ADM 104/159.

MEDALS

Campaign and gallantry medals for Naval personnel are largely the same as for the other services and are described in Chapter 2.

Recommendations for gallantry medals to members of the Royal Navy and Royal Marines are in ADM 1/29358-30077, 30098-30984 (with an index in ADM 12) and ADM 116 at Kew. They also include some awards to members of the Merchant Navy and the RAF. Lists of naval recipients of the Victoria and George crosses are in ADM 1/23187 and George Medal (GM) in ADM 171/164-165.

Lists of men who were awarded gallantry medals, together with service number and date the event was gazetted, can be found in the appropriate volume of: *Seedie's Roll of Naval Honours and Awards 1939-1959* (Ripley Registers 1989), *Seedie's list of Coastal Forces Awards for World War II* (Ripley Registers 1992), *Seedie's List of Submarine Awards for World War II* (Ripley Registers 1990). TNA Library has the volume for Submarines.

NAVAL AWARDS

Details of ratings who were awarded the Conspicuous Gallantry Medal (CGM) are listed in P. McDermott, *For Conspicuous Gallantry – the Register of the Conspicuous Gallantry Medal, 1855-1958* (Naval and Military Press, 1998). Medal rolls for the Distinguished Service Cross (DSC) are in ADM 171/164-165, and a similar list for officers of the RNR is in BT 164/23.

Medal rolls for the Distinguished Service Medal (DSM) from 1942 only are also to be found in ADM 171/164-165. However, all recipients are listed in W.H. Fevyer, *The Distinguished Service Medal 1939-1946* (Hayward, 1981). Lists of men who were awarded the Long Service and Good Conduct Medal during the war are in ADM 171.

The service records for the Royal Naval Reserve contain papers on awards to RNR officers. These documents are in BT 164.

CASUALTIES

KILLED OR MISSING IN ACTION

The main sources for casualties during the war are described in Chapter 2. There are, however, several sources specifically for the Royal Navy, the most important of which are two typescript lists held by the Department of Printed Books at the Imperial War Museum: *Names of Officers who Died during the Period beginning 3rd September 1939 and ending 30th June 1948* and the *Register of Deaths (Naval Ratings) 3rd September 1939 to 30th June 1948*. A set is also with the Royal Naval Museum in Portsmouth (addresses in Appendix I). Servicemen are listed by surname, together with official number, branch of service, ship, and date and place of birth and death, and occasionally details of medals awarded or other information.

Reports of deaths of individuals are to be found at Kew in series ADM 104/127-139, for naval ratings, and ADM 104/105-107, arranged by ship for deaths other than those from enemy action. Again, details of service number, ship, and place and date of birth and death (and its cause) are given.

A list of RNR officers killed or wounded during the war is in BT 164/23. Details of RNR and RNVR medical officers who were killed between 1939 and 1946 are in ADM 261/1. In addition there is a microfiche set of the General Register Office's registers of deaths between 1939 and 1948 in the Microfilm Reading Room.

SICK AND WOUNDED

Surgeons' journals, compiled by doctors on board ships and at some hospitals can be found in series ADM 101 at Kew. These journals contain an account of the treatment of medical and surgical cases, and usually a copy of the daily sick list, statistical abstracts of the incidence of diseases, and general comments on the health and activities of the ship's company. They are arranged by ship or shore station. ADM 261/1 also includes reports of medical treatment to survivors of RN ships either sunk or badly damaged by enemy action.

PRISONERS OF WAR

In addition to the records described in Chapter 2, there are several other sources for naval PoWs. Lists of Royal Navy personnel interned in enemy camps may be found in many of the files in ADM 1 (code 79) and ADM 116 (code 79) at Kew, although the exact files are not identifiable from the catalogue. A list of Fleet Air Arm prisoners of war in Germany and occupied Europe can be found at www.fleetairarmarchive.net/RollofHonour/PoW/Camp_list.htm.

OPERATIONAL RECORDS

Operational records can be found in three major TNA series:

- ADM 199 – Case papers relating to all sorts of naval activities from convoys to captains' reports on damage done to individual ships.

A mess on board HMS Ark Royal. *(From O Rutter,* Ark Royal, *HMSO, 1942)*

- ADM 1 – Admiralty and Secretariat Papers – arranged by subject (called codes).
- ADM 116 – More secret and important papers gathered by the Admiralty and bound together in cases. As with ADM 1, they are arranged by subject codes.

In practice there seems to be no hard and fast rule about which records are to be found where, although it is best to start by going through ADM 199. Fortunately, TNA's online catalogue can make the search much simpler than was once the case. There are card indexes in the Research Enquiries Room to convoys (arranged by convoy number) and operation codenames, and a subject card index to the material found in ADM 199. More information can be found in a TNA research guide, *Royal Navy: Operational Records: Second World War, 1939-1945*. A list of actions in which the Navy was engaged can be found in Gordon Smith, *The War at Sea: Royal and Dominion Navy Actions in World War 2* (Ian Allen, 1989).

DUNKIRK

The Caird Library, at the National Maritime Museum, has a large collection relating to the retreat from Dunkirk in 1940. In particular it has *The Dunkirk List. Dunkirk Withdrawal: Operation Dynamo May 26-June 4, 1940: Alphabetical List of Vessels Taking Part, With Their Services*, which was compiled by Lt. Col. G.P. Orde immediately after the evacuation was completed, using all available sources, official and private, including numerous interviews with survivors. Orde gives an account of every vessel taking part in Operation Dynamo, arranged in alphabetical order by name. Some general subject headings are included in the sequence, such as 'blockships', 'flare burning drifters', 'minesweeper groups', and 'routes to Dunkirk', and cross-references are given where necessary.

SHIPS' LOGS

Ships' logs constitute a ship's official record, containing information about routine shipboard activities at sea and in harbour, as well as weather and sea conditions, all movements of the ship, details of operational exercises and special events such as visits by senior military personnel. Little or no personal information about individuals is entered in these records. Ships' logs are in series ADM 53 at Kew, although ones for ships smaller than cruisers do not appear to have survived, apart for 1939 and the early months of 1940. It is easy to find out which logs are available by typing the name of the vessel into TNA's online catalogue (www.nationalarchives.gov.uk/catalogue).

SHIPS' MOVEMENTS

It is fairly easy to trace a ship's movements (including those of Allied countries) by using one of a series of lists at Kew:

- Pink Lists (ADM 187): Regularly printed lists, usually compiled every three or four days, showing where each ship was stationed or their movements, with dates of arrival and departure.
- Red Lists (ADM 208): Weekly lists of all minor vessels in home waters, arranged by command.
- Blue Lists (ADM 209): Ships under construction.
- Green Lists (ADM 210): Weekly lists of landing craft and similar vessels in home waters and foreign stations, arranged by command.

CAPTAIN'S LETTERS AND REPORTS OF PROCEEDINGS

These contain information relating to the activities of naval vessels, in the form of letters from the commanding officer (Captain's Letters) or Reports of Proceedings (R of P), submitted to the Admiralty. These are probably the most informative source if you are researching a particular incident. Unfortunately they are not found together in a single source, but are scattered through ADM 1 and ADM 199. You may find them arranged by ship or by operation or convoy.

OTHER RECORDS RELATING TO SHIPS

Brief histories of RN ships are to be found in J.J. Colledge and Ben Warlow, *Ships of the Royal Navy: The Complete Record of All Fighting Ships of the Royal Navy from the Fifteenth Century to the Present* (Greenhill Books, 2003). On a more melancholy note, John M. Young, *Britain's Sea War: A Diary of Ship Losses, 1939-1945* (Patrick Stephens, 1989) lists all ships, military and civilian, lost during the war. It is based on two official government publications:

The White Ensign flies proudly on HMS Ark Royal*: (From O Rutter,* Ark Royal, *HMSO, 1942)*

Ships of the Royal Navy: Statement of Losses during the Second World War (HMSO, 1947) and *British Merchant Vessels Lost or Damaged by Enemy Action during the Second World War* (HMSO, 1947). Copies should be available in large reference libraries as well as at TNA and naval museums. Brief descriptions of each RN ship lost, and the reason for its loss, can be found at www.naval-history.net.

A card index can be found in the Research Enquiries Room to TNA references for individual ships and submarines. A court martial was held after the loss of a ship and these records are for the most part in ADM 1, although they are closed for 75 years.

Photographs of Naval ships are in series ADM 176 at TNA, although larger and better collections are held by the National Maritime Museum and the Imperial War Museum. The Royal Naval Museum also has the Wright and Logan Collection of warship photographs which consists of around 22,000 negatives, mostly on glass plates, of ships from 1924 to 1998. Indeed the NMM and the Royal Naval Museum have many records relating to individual naval ships.

There are a number of websites dedicated to specific RN ships, such as the one for the battleship HMS *Rodney* at www.geocities.com/Pentagon/Quarters/4433, which includes crew lists as well as photographs and a history of the ship.

OTHER NAVAL SERVICES

NAVAL RESERVES

Unlike the other services, the several Naval reserve forces were not fully absorbed into the Royal Navy and maintained something of a separate nature. The history of the men who served in them is told in Stephen Howarth, *The Royal Navy's Reserves in War and Peace 1903-2003* (Leo Cooper, 2003). The reserve services were:

- *Royal Naval Reserve* (RNR) which was made up of men and officers from the Merchant Navy. As a result, many of the records are to be found in the Board of Trade (BT) series of records at TNA. An important section of the Reserve was the Royal Naval Patrol Service (sometimes nicknamed 'Harry Tate's Navy') recruited largely from fishermen who manned small vessels such as minesweepers. Two websites devoted to the Patrol Service are www.harry-tates.org.uk and www.rnps.lowestoft.org.uk. An interesting site devoted to specific individuals' wartime service with the RNR is at www.royal-naval-reserve.co.uk/research.htm.
- *Royal Naval Volunteer Reserve* (RNVR) was comprised of men from all walks of life, who trained with the Navy at weekends in peacetime. During the war the majority of officers were granted commissions in the Reserve. There were also various branches for specialists, including chaplains, accountants and engineers. It is sometimes referred to as the 'Wavy Navy' because of the waved gold rings worn by RNR officers on their cuffs to denote rank.

FLEET AIR ARM

The Fleet Air Arm was finally transferred from the Air Ministry to the Admiralty in 1937. In September 1939, the Fleet Air Arm consisted of 20 squadrons and 232 aircraft on strength. The war gave a new impetus to naval flying which gradually changed naval tactics from a ship versus ship conflict to aircraft versus ships, often with devastating effects. The crippling of the Italian Fleet in Taranto Harbour by Swordfish biplanes carrying torpedoes in a night attack in 1940 was undoubtedly the most notable Fleet Air Arm success of the war, although the FAA served in almost every theatre, taking part in the Battles of France and Britain, Battle of Atlantic, Russian convoys, invasion of Madagascar, North African and Libyan campaigns, invasions of Italy, and Southern France, D-Day, the Pacific and the planned invasion of Japan.

The FAA was also instrumental in sinking the greatest tonnage of enemy shipping, and was one of the main weapons against the U-boat. FAA aircrew were also adept at aerial combat and had many air aces, and received numerous honours including two Victoria Crosses, and many Distinguished Service Orders, Distinguished Service Crosses, Distinguished Service Medals and Mentions in Despatches. In September 1945 the strength of the Fleet Air Arm was: 59 aircraft carriers, 3,700 aircraft, 72,000 officers and men and 56 air stations all over the world. The aircraft carrier had replaced the battleship as the Fleet's capital ship and its aircraft were strike weapons in their own right.

Personnel records are with the Ministry of Defence, details can be found in Chapter 2. Combat reports compiled by pilots are in AIR 50 at Kew. A roll of honour for FAA officers and ratings who lost their lives during the war can be found at www.fleetairarmarchive.net/RollofHonour/Index.html. The FAA Memorial Chapel is St Bartholomew's church, Yeovilton near the FAA Museum in Somerset. An (incomplete) list of honours and awards made to Fleet Air Arm personnel can be found in William Chatterton Dickson, *Seedie's List of Fleet Air Arm Awards 1939-1969* (Ripley Registers 1990). A copy is in TNA Library and can be found at other museums and large reference libraries. An online list of gallantry awards and how to find out more about them is at: www.fleetairarmarchive.net. Some FAA personnel received RAF awards and you may need to go through the records described in Chapter 6.

Fleet Air Arm squadrons were assigned numbers between 700-899 and 1700-1899. Surviving Operations Record Books of Fleet Air Arm squadrons are in ADM 207 with a few in AIR 27 at TNA. Line books (basically more informative and personal ORBs) and much other information about individual squadrons (and indeed individual members of the Arm and the aircraft they flew) can be found at the Fleet Air Arm Museum's Centre for Naval Aviation Records and Research (see Appendix I for address).

Reports of Proceedings about missions and operations compiled by commanding officers are with those of ships and squadrons in ADM 199 and elsewhere at Kew. As the FAA worked closely with RAF Coastal Command, it may be worth checking headquarters papers in AIR 15 and Operations Record Books in AIR 24. No Aircraft Carrier Flying Log Books are known to have survived.

A superb website devoted to the FAA is www.fleetairarmarchive. net. On it you can a find a roll of honour, lists of FAA prisoners of war, histories of squadrons, job descriptions for the technical and support staff, and biographies of notable pilots. Two informative books are: John Winton, *Find, Fix and Strike! The FAA at War 1939-45* (BT Batsford, 1980) and Ray Sturtivant and Theo Balance, *The Squadrons of the Fleet Air Arm* (Air Britain (Historians) Ltd, 1994) which provides a brief history for each FAA squadron, listing aircraft types flown, where based and commanding officers.

ROYAL FLEET AUXILIARY

Formed in 1905, the Royal Fleet Auxiliary (RFA) is responsible for resupplying Naval vessels. Crew members are merchant seamen and officers. Seamen's pouches (or files) for seamen who served with the RFA are in series BT 390 at TNA. For more information see Chapter 5.

ROYAL MARINES

The Royal Marines traditionally were soldiers who fought on the sea, manning ships' guns or leading raiding parties on the enemy's shore. During the Second World War some 80,000 men served in the Royal Marines, and they continued to operate at sea and in land formations, but 1942 saw the formation of the first Royal

Marines Commandos. No 5 RM Commandos were amongst the first to land on D-Day, and two thirds of all the landing craft involved were crewed by Royal Marines. 16,000 members of the Corps took part in Operation Overlord in many roles, some even manning tanks. Others took part in seaborne raids in Norway, elsewhere in Europe and in Burma.

The Royal Marines are a self-contained body administered by the Admiralty, and this leads to a certain amount of confusion and overlap. Officers, for example, have Army ranks, but receive the pay and allowances of their Naval equivalents. Service records are still held by the Royal Navy. The address is given in Chapter 2.

War diaries for RM units, including the Commandos, are in ADM 202 at Kew. There is some overlap with war diaries for combined operations in DEFE 2. Some files about the award of gallantry medals to Commandos are in ADM 1. Registers of Marine Deaths are in ADM 104/127-139. A list of Royal Marines known to have been held in German camps between 1939 and 1945 is to be found in ADM 201/111.

Much information about the history of the Corps is held in the Library of the Royal Marines Museum (see Appendix I for details), They also have an extensive collection of photographs, operational war diaries and other reports. More about tracing Marine ancestors can be found in Garth Thomas, *Records of Royal Marines* (PRO Publications, 1994), although it does not say very much about the Second World War. A detailed history of the Corps is Julian Thompson, *The Royal Marines: from Soldiers to Special Force* (Sidgwick and Jackson, 2000). On the internet, www.royalmarines.org is an interesting site although there is relatively little about the Corps' history during the Second World War. A brief history of the Corps can be found at www.regiments.org/regiments/uk/specfor/RM.htm with a very good reading list of books about the Marines.

THE SUBMARINE SERVICE

In general, records for submarines and submariners are very similar to those of the rest of the Navy. Submarine logs are in ADM 173 at TNA, which record all wheel, telegraph and depth keeping orders, and details of battery charges, torpedo firing and navigation. They were kept by crew members otherwise engaged in steering or depth keeping, and contain many abbreviated references. Some logs are humorously annotated with notes and drawings. War patrol reports and associated records, arranged by boat, are in ADM 236, with some records in ADM 199.

The Royal Navy Submarine Museum has substantial archives of papers, both official and private, relating to the service. Of particular interest is the material relating to individual vessels. Contact: The Royal Navy Submarine Museum, Haslar Jetty Road, Gosport PO12 2A; tel: 023 9252 9217; www.rnsubmus.co.uk. The website also has pages devoted to the loss of individual submarines at sea.

John Atkinson, *Royal Navy Submarine Service Losses in WWII* (Galago, 2004) is a comprehensive record of the names of all the men who lost their lives during submarine service. The book includes details of each submarine lost (from HMS/m *Oxley* in 1939 to HMS/m *Porpoise* in 1945), the reason, date and the commanding officer, together with each member of the crew who died, his name, rank and any decorations awarded.

WOMEN'S ROYAL NAVAL SERVICE

In 1939, Mrs Vera Laughton Mathews, who had served with the WRNS during the First World War, was invited to become Director of the WRNS for the Second World War. By 1944, the service numbered 74,000 women undertaking a variety of 200 different jobs. Many Wrens were involved in the planning and organisation of naval operations, as well as maintenance. Thousands of women served overseas and large numbers served in other branches of the Navy, such as the Fleet Air Arm, Coastal Forces, Combined Operations and the Royal Marines. During the war, the service lost 303 women due to enemy action.

Service records are still with the Ministry of Defence (see Chapter 2 for details), although cards and files for some officers can be found in ADM 340. The National Archives has some other records, mainly to do with the administration of the service, in ADM 1. The Royal Naval Museum (see Appendix I for address) houses a comprehensive WRNS archive, containing materials relating to the history of the service. It has official and unofficial documents, personal manuscripts, photographs, uniforms and artefacts for the full existence of the service.

5

THE MERCHANT MARINE

SERVICE RECORDS

OFFICERS

Chronological registers of the issue, or reissue, of certificates of competence are to be found at Kew in:

- **BT 317** Registers of Masters and Mates Certificates Passings and Renewal (1917-1977).
- **BT 318** Registers of Examinations for Certificates of Masters, Mates and Engineers, Returns of Passings and Failures (1928-1981).
- **BT 369** Registers of Passes and Renewals of Certificates of Competency for Fishing Officers (Skippers and 2nd hands) 1883-1959.

LLOYD'S CAPTAINS' REGISTERS

Lloyd's Captains' Registers extend the date and amount of information available for masters. They were compiled from the record of certificates issued to foreign-going masters, which was kept by the Registrar General of Shipping and Seamen.

The information was arranged in an alphabetical sequence, known as Captains' Registers. An incomplete set of Captains' Registers can be seen on microfilm at TNA: they list, for each person: name, place and year of birth; date, number and place of issue of master's certificates; other special qualifications; name and number (taken from the Mercantile Navy Lists) of each ship; date of engagement and discharge as master or mate; the destination of each voyage; casualties; any special awards (e.g. war service). The originals are at Guildhall Library (see Appendix I for address). More information can be found in a Guildhall Library leaflet, *Lloyd's Captains' Registers*, available at www.history.ac.uk/gh/capreg.htm, and a TNA research guide, *Merchant Seamen: Officers' Service Records 1845-1965*.

SEAMEN

There are two series of records which you may need to consult so it is reasonably important to know when your man left the service.

The Fourth Register (Central Indexed Register) was started in October 1913 and continued until 1941. Copies of the registry cards are on microfiche at The National Archives.

The original cards are held by Southampton City Archive, South Block Basement, Civic Centre, Southampton SO14 7LY; tel: 023 8083 2251; www.southampton.gov.uk/leisure/archives/collections/records-of-merchant-seamen.asp#0. At the time of writing there is a charge of £5 per search.

The full register consists of four sets of cards, held in four separate record series. These include details of all categories of men and women employed at sea.

In 1941 the Essential Work (Merchant Navy) Order created a Merchant Navy Reserve Pool. To ensure that seamen would always be available to crew vessels, the Government paid them to remain in the Reserve Pool when they were ashore. For the first time, continuous paid employment instead of casual work was available to all seamen, and comprehensive and effective registration became possible. All those who had served at sea during the previous five years, and those who were intending to serve during the war, were required to register. A new Central Register of Seamen (known as the Fifth Register of Seamen) was established, whose records are now largely at TNA. Cards for seamen who were still serving in 1941 were removed from the old Fourth Register, placed in pouches (BT 372) or files (BT 364) and their details add to the new register in BT 382. The Fifth Register was maintained until 1972.

The seamen's pouches in BT 372 consist of an individual's papers filed together in paper envelopes known as 'pouches'. The contents vary from single registry cards to ID cards, photographs, letters,

A merchant seaman practises his gunnery. (From Warren Armstrong, Battle of the Oceans, *Jarrolds, 1943)*

applications forms and other ephemera. The records cover the period 1913 to 1972, though few have contents dating further back than the 1930s. Pouches for men who served on RN auxiliary vessels are in BT 390, while others for men who served in the liberation of Europe are in BT 391. Conversely some material that might have been expected to be in pouches is in BT 364.

Unfortunately not every pouch survives. However, those which do are arranged by individual in the TNA online catalogue (www.nationalarchives.gov.uk/catalogue), so it is easy to check. Entries contain the Discharge 'A' number, surname, initials, and in the majority of cases, date of birth and place of birth. Detailed instructions, with examples of how to use these records, are given in a TNA online Research Guide: *Merchant Seamen: Sea Service Records 1913-1972*.

A social history of the life of merchant seamen during the war is Bernard Edwards, *The Quiet Heroes: British Merchant Seaman at War* (Leo Cooper, 2002). An interesting website telling the story of an individual merchant seaman is http://wardjc.com/WW2Memories.htm.

MEDALS

CAMPAIGN MEDALS

At the conclusion of the Second World War medal papers were created which included details of a seaman's service. They were signed by the individual as to the accuracy of the information, and then returned to the Registry of Shipping and Seamen (RSS). Medals were not automatically issued but had to be claimed by the veteran. These papers are still retained by the RSS but are not complete.

Series BT 395 at Kew contains a database to the Second World War medals issued to merchant seamen between 1946 and 2002 for both medals claimed and those actually issued. It gives details of the ribbons and medals issued to individual seamen for their service. The data records each seaman's name with, usually, his discharge book number and date and place of birth, as well as the medals, ribbons and clasps issued together with a reference to the medal papers file. The database is now available online and can be searched at www.documentsonline.nationalarchives.gov.uk,

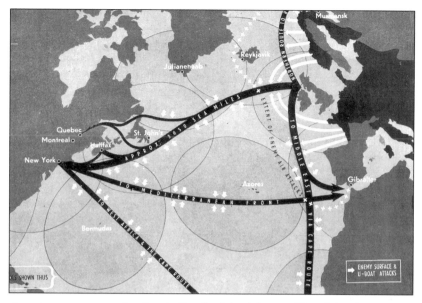

A contemporary map showing the Battle of the Atlantic. (From Merchantmen at War: The Official Story of the Merchant Navy 1939-1944, *HMSO, 1944)*

although there is a fee (currently £3.50) to download an individual record.

If you are trying to discover whether a medal was issued, or there was an unclaimed entitlement, then the RSS should be contacted as they have the most up-to-date records. To prove entitlement you will normally need to show that either a man was in service for the prescribed period of time (normally six months) or that the vessel on which he served entered the related theatre of war. This can be done by searching the records described above. The RSS also hold the actual applications for campaign medals: Registry of Shipping and Seamen, Anchor Court, Keen Road, Cardiff CF24 5JW; tel: 029 2044 8800; email: rss@mcga.gov.uk.

GALLANTRY MEDALS

Lists of men who were awarded gallantry medals, together with service number and the date the event was gazetted, can be found in: *Seedie's List of Awards to the Merchant Navy for World War II* (Ripley Registers, 1997).

There are a number of other sources at The National Archives which may help if you are researching an award. Details of medal winners of the Albert and George medals can be found in BT 339/5. Code 6 of Marine Correspondence and Papers in series MT 9 contains many files relating to various awards, including the Board of Trade Medal for Gallantry in Saving Life at Sea, the Sea Transport Medal, the George Medal, Lloyd's Medal for Gallantry at Sea and the Polish Cross of Valour.

The Lloyd's Medal for Gallantry at Sea was instituted by the Committee of Lloyd's in December 1940, to be awarded to officers and men of the Merchant Navy and Fishing Fleet in cases of exceptional gallantry at sea in time of war. Jim Gawler, *Lloyd's Medals, 1836-1989: A History of Medals Awarded by The Corporation of Lloyd's* (Hart Publishing, 1989) describes the medal and includes a list of winners. A copy is in The National Archives Library.

Many merchant navy officers and men received naval gallantry awards during the Second World War. Records of these can be found in code 85 in series ADM 1 and ADM 199. More details about the award of medals, both campaign and gallantry, can be found in the research guide *Merchant Seamen: Medals and Honours* to be found on TNA website.

CASUALTIES

KILLED OR MISSING IN ACTION

The sacrifice made by merchant seamen during the war, particularly during the Battle of the Atlantic and 1942 and 1943, has sometimes been overlooked. But as the eminent military historian John Keegan once remarked: 'The 30,000 men of the British Merchant Navy who fell victim to the U-boats between 1939 and 1945, the majority drowned or killed by exposure on the cruel North Atlantic sea, were quite as certainly front-line warriors as the guardsmen and fighter pilots to whom they ferried the necessities of combat. Neither they nor their American, Dutch, Norwegian or Greek fellow mariners wore uniform and few have any memorial. They stood nevertheless between the Wehrmacht and the domination of the world.'

Merchant seamen who died at sea are recorded by the Commonwealth War Graves Commission in the same way as other seamen. For details see Chapter 2. The names of 24,000 seamen and women who lost their lives are commemorated on the Tower Hill Memorial in the City of London (nearly opposite Tower underground station). The Memorial Register, listing everybody who appears on the memorial, may be consulted at Trinity House Corporation, Trinity Square (Cooper's Row entrance), Tower Hill, London EC3 N4DH, which will be found behind the Memorial; tel: 020 7481 6900.

A roll of honour for men who lost their lives was compiled after the war by the Board of Trade; it is now in series BT 339 at Kew, arranged both by individual and by ship.

PRISONERS OF WAR

There is an extensive collection of records in series BT 373 at Kew, giving the circumstances of capture and the eventual fate of British and Allied Asian merchant seamen captured during the Second World War.

There are pouches for individual seamen which are searchable by name in TNA's online catalogue. Each pouch typically contains the name of the ship lost; a card or form containing circumstantial details (including PoW camp and number, full name, date and place of birth, number, rank or rating, name and details of ship, next of kin, address and country of detention); Prisoner of War Branch PC 96 (postal censorship) forms vetting messages to and from family and friends; Envelope RS3 which usually has notes of release from captivity/repatriation written on it where appropriate. Some pouches may also contain personal letters to and from prisoners of war. Collective alphabetical listings of prisoners (as opposed to individual pouches) are contained in BT 373/3717-3722. For details of men who died in captivity in Japan and Germany, try BT 373/3720-3721.

BT 373 also includes details of ships captured or lost due to enemy action. These contain miscellaneous papers relating to the circumstances of loss/capture. Again you can search for a ship by using the online catalogue.

Pieces in another series, BT 382/3232-3249 consist of an alphabetical series of printed cards relating to merchant seamen prisoners of all nationalities. The cards normally give details of: camp and PoW number; surname and full forenames; date and place of birth; discharge 'A' number and rank/rating; details of ship; next-of-kin and relationship; home address. In addition, some

Many crew members, generally referred to as lascars, came from the Empire such as here from Bombay, Sierra Leone and Mombasa. (From Merchantmen at War: The Official Story of the Merchant Navy 1939-1944, *HMSO, 1944)*

include dates of death, exchange, repatriation and arrival back in the United Kingdom. General correspondence on British merchant seamen taken prisoner is in MT 9 (code 106).

Of the 5,000 Allied merchant seamen captured by the Germans some 4,500 were at some time held at the camp Marlag und Milag Nord, Westertimke, near Bremen, Germany (Marlag held Royal Navy personnel and Milag Merchant seamen). A camp history is in WO 208/3270.

More details can be found in a TNA Research Guide: *Prisoners of War, British: 1939-1953.*

OPERATIONAL RECORDS

RECORDS OF SHIPS

The basic source of information is the annual *Lloyd's Register of Shipping* (for ships of all nations), and to a lesser extent the *Mercantile Navy List* (just for British ships) which was published only for 1939 and 1940. The *Register* describes, classifies and registers vessels according to certain criteria of physical structure and equipment, to enable underwriters, shipbrokers, and shipowners more easily to

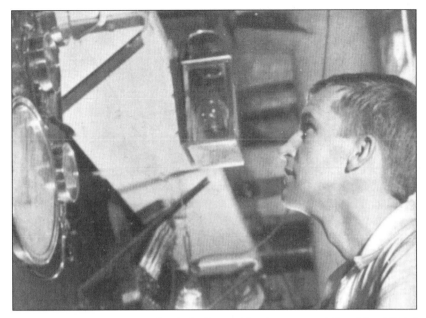

An engineer concentrates on his dials. (From Merchantmen at War: The Official Story of the Merchant Navy 1939-1944, *HMSO, 1944)*

assess commercial risk and to negotiate marine insurance rates. It is published mid-year and covers ships registered between 1 July and 30 June of the previous year. Some ships, however, were too short-lived to be included, and some foreign-registered vessels were omitted from the Register because of the difficulty of gathering information in wartime. Copies of the Register are to be found in the Research Enquiries Room at Kew, the Guildhall Library and the National Maritime Museum (addresses in Appendix I). An introduction to the Register can be found at www.mariners-l.co.uk/reslloydsregister.htm.

Merchant Shipping Movement Cards at Kew, in series BT 389, give the name of a ship and details of its movements, namely, the ports at which it docked, and passage between ports. They also record the location (by latitude and longitude) and date a ship was sunk. It should be noted that the cards do not always reflect changes in the ship's name and that it may be necessary to search for a ship under its various names.

Other useful sources are crew agreements and log books (where they survive), which are in BT 380 and BT 381 (for ships trading around the coasts of the British Isles). There is an index showing which records are to be found where in BT 385, arranged by ship. Crew agreements list all members of the crew. Log books list daily occurrences and may include telegrams and other paperwork. Unfortunately these records were often destroyed when a vessel sank as the result of enemy action.

Ships employed on Government service are shown in two series of the Admiralty Service Lists which give dates and type of ships' duties. Sets can be found at TNA in series MT 65/333-334, 467-469 and (for small craft) ADM 199/2429-2432, at the National Maritime Museum and no doubt in other specialist reference libraries. Other records relating to ships may sometimes be found in the surviving records of shipping companies. You can find which records are held where by using TNA's National Register of Archives (www.nationalarchives.gov.uk/nra).

CONVOYS

A convoy can be defined as 'one or more merchant ships sailing under escort by naval ships'. The average convoy consisted of between six and nine columns of ships with five ships in each column. The largest ever was HX 300 which had 167 ships sailing in 19 columns. The HX series was also the longest running convoy series, starting from the 16th September 1939 with HX 1, and finishing with HX 358 on the 23rd May 1945. Convoys were referred to by a letter and number code. The letters would normally stand for the port of departure, and the port of destination, the numbers denoting the amount of previous convoys in that system. All in all there were 452 different series throughout the war. Examples were: AB (Aden to Bombay), AG (Alexandria to Greece), HX (Halifax-Liverpool, and VT (Valletta to Tripoli).

'Convoy Packs', in series ADM 237 at Kew, are convoy records which include reports of proceedings, commodores' reports and other papers. About half this series was destroyed. References are included in the convoy card indexes in the Research Enquiries Room at Kew. Other reports, generally referred to by their convoy number, are in ADM 199.

Arnold Hague, *The Allied Convoy System, 1939-1945: Its*

An aerial view of a convoy, showing how close the ships were to each other. (From Warren Armstrong, Battle of the Oceans, *Jarrolds, 1943)*

Organisation, Defence and Operation (Chatham Press, 2003), provides a detailed account of the convoy system. Also included is an appendix listing every North Atlantic-related convoy, with details of departure and arrival dates and the ships involved, and an index of ships lost.

The loss of merchant vessels is recorded in the Daily Casualty Registers now in series BT 347 at Kew to which there is a microfiched card index (BT 347/8). This index also provides useful references to *Lloyd's List*. Copies are to be found at the Guildhall Library, the National Maritime Museum and other places. Probably the best place to start, however, is by consulting Alan J. Tennet, *British and Commonwealth Merchant Ship Losses to Axis Submarines 1939-1945* (Sutton, 2001), which describes the sinking of each ship, the master's name and fate of the crew. It is based, in part, on the official British Government publication *British Merchant Vessels Lost or Damaged by Enemy Action during the Second World War* (HMSO, 1947).

Two websites devoted to the Merchant Marine with lots about convoys are www.british-merchant-navy.co.uk and www.mikekemble.com/ww2/merchantnavy.html.

6

TRACING AIRMEN AND RAF OFFICERS

SERVICE RECORDS

Service records for airmen and officers have not been released, but can be accessed by veterans and their next of kin; details in Chapter 2. A summary of sources at The National Archives can be found in an online research guide, *Royal Air Force: Second World War, 1939-1945: Service Records,* available at www.catalogue. nationalarchives.gov.uk/RdLeaflet.asp?sLeafletID=61.

Biographical details of 1,200 fighter aces (that is, pilots who shot down five or more enemy aircraft) are given in C.F. Shores and C. Williams, *Aces High, the Fighter Aces of the British and Commonwealth Air Forces in World War Two* (2 vols, Grub Street, 1994, 1998). There are short biographies of 3,000 men who flew with Fighter Command during the Battle of Britain in K. Wynn, *Men of the Battle of Britain* (2nd edn, CCB Associates, 1999). Another book, Francis K. Mason's *Battle over Britain* (Aston Publications, 1990) also contains full details of all RAF Fighter Command flying personnel during the Battle of Britain, and their subsequent service history.

Details of pilots who served with 41 Squadron can be found at http://brew.clients.ch/Body41.htm. There are undoubtedly similar websites for other squadrons. An interesting site hosted by 207 Squadron Association is a list of names posted by former comrades and others seeking information on former RAF wartime personnel: www.rafinfo.org.uk/airsearch. An Air Force-wide site is www.worldwar2exraf.co.uk. It contains much more than lists of names, such as brief histories of individual squadrons and units.

The National Archives (TNA) has a selection of aircrew flying log books, recording all flights made, in series AIR 4. Often they are annotated with drawings or photographs. Other log books may be found in private or family papers or perhaps donated to museums and archives. More about private papers can be found in Chapter 2.

OFFICERS

Details of officers in the RAF, together with the branch they served with and details of promotions, appear in the *Air Force Lists*, which were published on a restricted basis six times a year during the war (quarterly in 1945). Sets are to be found in TNA's Microfilm Reading Room at Kew and at the RAF and Imperial War museums and possibly in other large reference libraries. Confidential lists were also produced with more detail and these can be found in series AIR 10 at TNA.

Submissions to the Sovereign for approval of appointments are in AIR 30. Many pieces concern honorary appointments for RAF personnel who were attached to the Royal Household. A website, www.rafweb.org, contains biographies of senior members of the RAF at Air Commodore level and above.

MEDALS

Campaign and gallantry medals for RAF personnel are largely the same as the other services and the major sources are described in Chapter 2.

Gallantry awards to RAF (and where appropriate, FAA) personnel were subdivided into two types: immediate (for single acts of bravery), or non-immediate, which were normally given at the conclusion of a tour of duty of between 25 and 30 operations. The most common gallantry medal awarded to aircrew was the Distinguished Flying Cross (DFC) – some 20,000 such medals were issued – and its equivalent for non-commissioned officers, the Distinguished Flying Medal (DFM). There are several books listing winners of these medals: Nicholas and Carol Carter, *The Distinguished Flying Cross and How it Was Won 1918-1995* (2 vols, Savannah Publications, 1998); I.T. Tavender, *The Distinguished Flying Medal: A Record of Courage 1918-1982* (2nd edition, Savannah Publications, 2004);

A young Blenheim pilot in the early years of the war. (From Bomber Command: The Air Ministry's Account of Bomber Command's Offensive against the Axis, *HMSO, 1941)*

I.T. Tavender, *The Distinguished Flying Medal Register for the Second World* War (2 vols, Savannah Publications, 2000).

Surviving recommendations for gallantry awards are in series AIR 2 at Kew. Those for the Victoria Cross are in AIR 2 (for 1939-1942); in AIR 2/5010 (for 1943-1944) and in AIR 2/5867 (for 1944-1946). The recommendations are not indexed, nor are they arranged in any logical way. Fortunately, somebody is devoting his leisure hours to indexing them; contact Paul Baillie, 14 Wheatfields, St Ives PE17 6D, paul.baillie@talk21.com. For more details see William Spencer's *Air Force Records for Family Historians* (PRO, 2000).

CASUALTIES AND PRISONERS OF WAR

KILLED OR MISSING IN ACTION

The main sources for casualties during the war are described in Chapter 2. There are, however, several sources specifically for the RAF.

The national memorial to the missing of the RAF and Commonwealth air forces is at Runnymede near Egham, overlooking the Thames. Some 20,300 men are commemorated here. The Debt of Honour Register (www.cwgc.org) will tell you on which panel a man's name can be found. A roll of honour for men of the RAF can be found at the RAF's own church, St Clement Danes on the Strand in central London. A visit to the church can be a very moving affair.

Rolls of honour for Bomber Command groups are displayed in the following cathedrals: Lincoln – 1 and 5 Groups; York Minster – 4 and 6 Groups, and those members of 7 Group who died while serving in the York area; Ely – 2, 3, 8 and 100 Groups. The RAF Museum holds copies of all but the roll for 2 Group. The National Archives has a roll of honour for 5 Group in piece AIR 14/2091. In addition, RAF stations, squadrons and squadron associations may well maintain a roll of honour, which may be available online.

The Air Historical Branch of the Ministry of Defence holds casualty records for RAF personnel killed, injured, reported missing or taken prisoner of war. Transcripts can be provided to relatives only.

An index to some 65,000 RAF war dead, known as *RAF War Dead 1939-48*, who were killed while serving overseas or over enemy territory between 1939 and 1948 is at the Family Records Centre on the ground floor (address in Appendix I). The index is arranged alphabetically and gives full name, rank, service number, unit and year of death. Commonwealth citizens are not included, unless they served with the RAF.

Two comprehensive books contain chronological listings of the losses in action of individual aircraft and aircrew: W.R. Chorley, *RAF Bomber Command Losses* (4 vols, Midland Counties Publications, 1992-1998) and N.L.R. Franks, *Fighter Command Losses* (3 vols, Midland Publishing, 1997-2000).

PRISONERS OF WAR

As well as the sources given in Chapter 2 there are a number of other places to look for RAF prisoners, including the correspondence of the Air Ministry in AIR 2 or AIR 20 at TNA. An alphabetical list of British and Dominion Air Force PoWs in German hands in 1944-1945 is in AIR 20/2336. Nominal rolls of prisoners in German camps are in AIR 40/263 -281, and AIR 40/1488-1491. A roll for Changi prison in Singapore is in AIR 40/1899-1906.

A substantial quantity of material concerning British and

WAAFs packing parachutes: vital but tricky work. (From Coastal Command, HMSO, 1943)

Commonwealth PoWs can be found in the Headquarters Papers of Bomber Command (series AIR 14) and in the Air Ministry's Directorate of Intelligence Papers (AIR 40). Aerial photographs of camps are in AIR 40/227-231. Lists and additional aerial photographs of PoW camps in Germany, Italy and Occupied Europe, including reports on transfers, are in AIR 14/1235-1240, and similar documentation on German camps occurs in AIR 40/227-231.

Reports on many individual RAF servicemen taken prisoner in occupied Europe, with the circumstances of their capture, are in AIR 14/470-471. Reports on the condition of British and Dominion PoWs in German and Japanese camps towards the end of the war occur in AIR 40/2361 and 2366.

Oliver Clutton-Brock, *Footprints in the Sands of Time - RAF Bomber Command Prisoners of War in Germany 1939-1945* (Grub Street, 2003) contains the full list of Bomber Command prisoners.

ESCAPE AND EVASION

A number of airmen either escaped or evaded capture. On their return to Britain they completed escape and evasion reports, which can be found in AIR 40/1874, or for the Far East AIR 40/2462. These reports and other material form the basis of Graham Pitchfork, *Shot Down and on the Run: The RAF and Commonwealth Aircrews who got home from behind enemy lines, 1940-1945* (TNA, 2003). The RAF Escapers Society's website (www.rafinfo.org.uk/rafescape) also has some useful pages.

Details of the RAF's Air Sea Rescue Service can be found in Graham Pitchfork's *Shot Down and in the Drink* (TNA, 2005).

OPERATIONAL RECORDS

OPERATION RECORD BOOKS

Operation Record Books (ORBs) are the most important and can be the most informative records you will use to trace a person's service in the RAF. These books were compiled on a daily basis by all RAF units. In fact, there were two types of ORB: monthly summaries (known as Form 540) and daily summaries (Form 541) which were generally compiled by operational squadrons. What was recorded inevitably varied, with the most comprehensive accounts generally for squadrons on active service. The records generally become fuller in 1942 and later. Inevitably, records for squadrons who flew in the Battle of Britain are sometimes scrappy. And sometimes records are missing entirely, for example for units in Malta which were under continual air attack. In the smaller units ORBs may not exist for the last months of the war as commanding or other officers may have taken them with them when they were demobilised.

As well as official happenings, such as visits by members of the Royal Family or the arrival of a new commanding officer, less formal events may be recorded, such as Christmas festivities or inter-unit sporting matches. Occasionally there may be more unusual entries – I once found a description of a French brothel (complete with prices) – or photographs of unit members.

Form 541s include summaries of missions flown, usually with a list of crew members. They were often completed by the squadron intelligence officer after each raid. By going through them day by day you can work out which sorties a man went on and what happened on them. In addition there may be appendices, which can record men posted in or posted out, and daily orders issued by the commanding officer.

The original Operation Record Books are at The National Archives in the following series: AIR 24 Commands, including Bomber and Fighter Commands; AIR 25 Groups; AIR 26 Wings; AIR 27 Squadrons; AIR 28 Stations; AIR 29 Miscellaneous units. In addition there are series for the South African Air Force (AIR 54) and Fleet Air Arm (ADM 207), which are described elsewhere.

Curiously, the ORBs do not seem to be widely copied or transcribed, so are not generally available outside The National Archives, but you may find extracts in unofficial unit histories or websites. As an example of what the records contain, you may like to look at the extracts from the ORB of the Communications Flight at RAF Habbaniya which came under Iraqi attack in May 1941, which can be found at http://skeet.worldonline.co.uk/index.html.

Based on entries in the ORBs and the daily summaries of events found in AIR 22, accounts of the daily operations of Bomber and Fighter Command can be found in: M. Middlebrook and C. Everitt, *The Bomber Command War Diaries* (Viking, 1985) and J. Foreman, *Fighter Command War Diaries, 1939-1945* (5 vols, Air Research Publications, 1996-2004). Summaries of squadron histories are also given in: J. Rawlings, *Fighter Squadrons of the RAF and their Aircraft* (Crecy Books, 1993); P. Moyes, *Bomber Squadrons of the RAF and their Aircraft* (Macdonald, 1976); J. Rawlings, *Coastal, Support and Special Squadrons of the RAF and their Aircraft* (Jane's, 1982).

COMBAT REPORTS

Combat reports were compiled by pilots after shooting down an enemy aircraft. They are a simple form containing the pilot's description of the action and where and when it took place. The reports are largely to be found in series AIR 50 at The National Archives. The RAF Museum has an incomplete set for fighter squadrons, although many are carbon copies and not necessarily easy to read. Not all combat reports survive. And where they do, several pilots may claim that they shot down a particular aircraft, so they should not always be taken as definite proof of a man's skill or heroism.

PLANNING AND ANALYSIS

The strategic conduct of the war was divided between the Air Ministry and various RAF commands, of which Bomber Command was the best known. Their records have long been available at The National Archives.

Material is sparsest for the first two years of the war, but by mid-1944 there are a multitude of reports and files on almost every aspect of the Air War. TNA's online catalogue (www.catalogue.nationalarchives.gov.uk) offers a fairly painless way to find papers on a certain operation, raid or technical development. Researchers should be warned that the titles of the files found in the catalogue may have only a tangential relation to the actual subject of the file itself. This is the legacy of the hurried transfer of files to the old Public Record Office in the early 1970s. In addition, many file titles only use operation codenames and abbreviations, so, for example, you may need to know what HUSKY and H2S mean. The most common codenames and abbreviations are given in Appendix III.

Series AIR 41 contains historical studies prepared by the Air Historical Branch after the war and may be a good place to start if you are looking at 'the big picture'. They cover most of the

A bomber crew being debriefed after a successful mission 'somewhere over Germany'. Summaries of these debriefings can be found in the Operation Record Books. (From Bomber Command: The Air Ministry's Account of Bomber Command's Offensive against the Axis, *HMSO, 1941)*

campaigns and theatres of the Second World War with the exceptions of the strategic air offensive and the Atlantic. British air defence and the Middle East campaign are extensively described.

The most useful Air Ministry series are: AIR 2 Air Ministry Registered Correspondence; AIR 8 Papers of the Chief of Air Staff; AIR 9 Director of Plans; AIR 10 Air Publications; AIR 19 Private

Office Papers, Secretary of State for Air; AIR 20 Air Ministry Unregistered Correspondence; AIR 22 Periodical returns, summaries and bulletins; AIR 34 Central Interpretation Unit (reconnaissance photographs); AIR 35 British Air Forces in France (1939-1940); AIR 37 Allied Expeditionary Air Force (North West Europe 1944-1945); AIR 40 Directorate of Intelligence; AIR 43 Combined Operations Planning Commmittee; AIR 72 Air Ministry Orders.

The papers of Commands are divided thus: AIR 13 Balloon Command; AIR 14 Bomber Command; AIR 15 Coastal Command; AIR 16 Fighter Command; AIR 17 Maintenance Command; AIR 23 Overseas Commands (largely those outside North West Europe); AIR 32 Training Command; AIR 38 Ferry and Transport Command; AIR 39 Army Co-operation Command.

Brief summaries of what can be found in each class are given in the Second World War section (by Roy Conyers Nesbit) in Simon Fowler et al, *RAF Records in the PRO* (Public Record Office, 1994) or TNA research guide *Royal Air Force: Operational Records*.

ORDERS OF BATTLE

There does not appear to be a central order of battle for the RAF, but orders can often be found in command papers (see above) and in series AIR 2 and AIR 20. Brief orders of battle are given in Ken Delve, *The Source Book of the RAF* (Airlife, 1994) and online at www.rafweb.org/Menu.htm.

C.G. Jefford, *RAF Squadrons* (Airlife, 1988) lists the airfields and aircraft used by individual squadrons, and also includes maps showing the locations of major airfields throughout the world at which these units have been based.

OTHER SOURCES

AIR HISTORICAL BRANCH

Any serious researcher into RAF history may need to contact the Air Historical Branch (RAF) at some stage of their studies: Air Historical Branch (RAF), Building 266, RAF Bentley Priory, Stanmore, Middlesex, HA7 3HH; www.raf.mod.uk/history/sources.html#archives. The Branch is a small working department of the Ministry of Defence, which seeks to maintain and preserve the historical memory of the RAF and to develop and encourage an informed understanding of RAF and air power history. They are not an archive, although they have a substantial archive of classified policy and operational documents, which are normally declassified after 30 years and transferred to The National Archives. The Branch also holds an index of RAF casualties from 1939 onwards, aircraft accident record cards dating from the inter-war years, and a photographic archive.

AIRCRAFT: GENERAL

There are huge numbers of books and websites devoted to aircraft design, construction and the flights they made, particularly for the famous planes ('warbirds' in the jargon) such as the Lancaster, Mosquito and Spitfire. The most correspondence we received when I was editor of *Family History Monthly* was when I wrongly captioned a photograph of a Westland Whirlwind. One reader who had flown it even sent in a complete history of the individual aircraft. There are some real obsessives out there! A useful general website giving aircraft specifications is www.warbirdsresourcegroup.org/BARC/index.html. Another site listing aircraft which flew in Bomber Command (among much else on the Command) is www.bomber-command.info.

AIRCRAFT MOVEMENTS AND CODES

It is generally possible to trace the RAF units to which a particular aircraft was allocated and the causes of any accidents in which it might have been involved. Operation Record Books can tell you more about the sorties a plane flew.

For every aircraft in the RAF, an Aircraft Movement Card (Air Ministry Form 78) was kept, recording the units to which that aeroplane was allocated and noting when it was damaged and repaired. Surviving cards are held by the Air Historical Branch, but the RAF Museum holds copies on microfilm and can supply prints for a small fee. Although most cards are quite informative, those for aircraft sent to the Middle and Far East theatres during the Second World War are not: the majority of these simply record the aircraft's arrival at its destination and make no mention of its subsequent fate.

The loneliest position on a bomber was the rear gunner 'Tail End Charlie'. Even in freezing conditions, he had to keep a constant watch on the skies for enemy fighter planes. (From Bomber Command: The Air Ministry's Account of Bomber Command's Offensive against the Axis, *HMSO, 1941)*

It is thought that similar records were kept by overseas commands, but these appear not to have survived.

M.J.F. Bowyer and J.D.R. Rawlings, *Squadron Codes 1937-56* (Patrick Stephens, 1979) gives the codes used by each squadron, flight or other unit to identify its aircraft. Codes are also listed in Ken Delve's *Source Book of the RAF* (Airlife, 1994).

AIRCRAFT ACCIDENTS AND LOSSES

Air Ministry Form 1180 was designed to record details of aircraft accidents so that the causes could be analysed and the resulting data used in accident prevention. The original cards are again with the Air Historical Branch, and the RAF Museum has microfilm copies which can be consulted, prints of which can be supplied (museum staff can supply limited numbers of transcripts/prints for postal enquirers). To trace a specific accident it is essential to know the date and the aircraft type – there are no indexes for location, unit or crew names. Again most serious accidents are noted in ORBs.

The records of inquiries into a few military aircraft accidents are in series AVIA 5 at TNA, although most pieces relate to civil aircraft. TNA has a small number of other records which might be of use. From January 1943 aircraft lost by Bomber Command are noted in the Missing Aircraft Register now to be found in piece AIR 14/2791. Other sources are in AIR 14/3466-3473, which contain 'K' reports submitted by survivors of bomber crews on the circumstances in which their aircraft were lost on operations. AIR 14/3213-3227 are raid plots – visual plots by returning aircrew of other aircraft seen to have been under attack or to have crashed, usually on night operations over Germany. These reports are often accompanied by positions marked on charts.

AIRFIELDS

It is possible to build up a history of individual airfields during the war from Station Record Books in series AIR 28 at Kew, and the ORBs for the squadrons and other units based at the airfield. General histories for many airfields and bases are given in a series of books from Countryside Books (www.countrysidebooks.co.uk). There may also be published histories of individual airfields and bases or websites devoted to them, particularly for the larger and important places. It is much more difficult to find anything about the construction of airfields. Few records are held at The National Archives – it is possible that the RAF Museum or Air Historical Branch may be able to help.

COURTS MARTIAL

The Judge Advocate General's Courts Martial Registers are in AIR 21. These give the name and rank of each prisoner, place of trial, nature of charge and sentence. The proceedings of district, general and field courts martial of officers and men of the RAF from 1941 are in AIR 18. Petitions to the Sovereign in court martial cases are in AIR 30.

RECONNAISSANCE PHOTOGRAPHS

During the Second World War, the Allied Central Interpretation Unit, based at Medmenham, was the headquarters of photographic intelligence. Like the code-breakers at Bletchley Park, with whom there are numerous similarities, the photographic interpreters played a key role in winning the war. No attack, whether a bombing raid, the landing of a few men on a beach or a massive landing of an army, was possible without the preparation of target material at the ACIU. The photographic techniques used allowed them to prepare highly detailed Interpretation Reports. For further information on Second World War photographic reconnaissance and intelligence, there is an article on the BBC website: www.bbc.co.uk/history/war/wwtwo/aerial_recon_gallery.shtml.

A selection of photographs can be found at Kew in series AIR 34. Of particular interest are the monthly *Evidence in Camera* booklets which were widely circulated within the RAF between October 1942 and March 1945. Most images, however, are with The Aerial Reconnaissance Archives (TARA), at Keele University. TARA charts the development of photographic reconnaissance and intelligence from a position of virtual insignificance during the early part of the Second World War to an integral part of Military Intelligence. Their largest catalogued archive is that of the Allied Central Interpretation Unit. Many of these images are available online (at least in theory) at www.evidenceincamera.co.uk. Unfortunately the site has rarely worked since it was launched in 2004 and at time of writing was still closed for maintenance work.

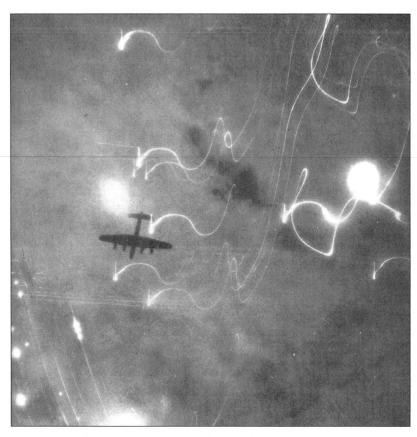

A Lancaster silhouetted in a photograph of bombs dropping during an air raid on a German city. (From Ernest Fairfax, Calling All Arms: the Story of How a Loyal Company of British Men and Women Lived Through Six Historic Years, *Hutchinson, 1945)*

AIR TRANSPORT AUXILIARY

The Air Transport Auxiliary (ATA) was a most unusual body consisting of civilian pilots who ferried aircraft from factories to the squadrons where they were needed. What's more, many members of the ATA were women. This led to a number of complaints. The view taken by C.G. Grey, editor of *Aeroplane*, was typical of the sentiment of the time:

We quite agree . . . that there are millions of women in the country who could do useful jobs in war. But the trouble is that so many of them insist on wanting to do jobs which they are quite incapable of doing. The menace is the woman who thinks that she ought to be flying in a high-speed bomber when she really has not the intelligence to scrub the floor of a hospital properly, or who wants to nose around as an Air Raid Warden and yet can't cook her husband's dinner. There are men like that so there is no need to charge us with anti-feminism. One of the most difficult types of man with whom one has to deal is that which has a certain amount of ability, too much self-confidence, an overload of conceit, a dislike of taking orders and not enough experience to balance one against the other by his own will. The combination is perhaps more common amongst women than men. And it is one of the commonest causes of crashes, in aeroplanes and other ways.

By the early part of 1940, the women pilots numbered 26. Throughout the war the women's Ferry Pool at Hamble delivered Spitfires from various factories as well as two- and four-engine aircraft. By September 1941, the ATA pilots were ferrying all types of operational aircraft. By the end of the war they had delivered 309,011 aircraft of more than 200 types. The wartime strength of the ATA was 1,152 men (including two of the author's uncles) and 600 women, including 166 pilots and flight engineers. The women pilots performed exactly the same duties as the men, and had equal pay and rights from late 1943.

Personnel records, including some logbooks, are at the RAF Museum. Other records are to be found in series AVIA 27 at TNA. An excellent account of one woman's career in the ATA is Diana Barnato Walker's *Spreading My Wings* (Grub Street, 2003). There are several interesting websites devoted to the ATA including: www.fleetairarmarchive.net/RollofHonour/ATA/ATA.html and www.airtransportaux.org.

WOMEN'S AUXILIARY AIR FORCE

The Women's Auxiliary Air Force (WAAF) was formed in June 1939 to take over some of the duties previously carried out by men. Numbers grew from about 1,700 members at the outbreak of war to approximately 180,000 by 1943. Service records can be accessed in exactly the same way as those for their male colleagues, and WAAF

WAAFs loading up a Short Sunderland flying boat. (From Coastal Command, *HMSO, 1943)*

activities are recorded in the appropriate ORB in AIR 28 (for stations) or AIR 29 (units). The Record Books for the Directorate of the WAAF are in AIR 24/1640-1646.

The WAAF Association's website has a comprehensive bibliography and other information about the Force – www.waafassociation.org.uk. A short book about the WAAF is Beryl E. Escott, *The WAAF* (Shire Publications, 2003). The author also wrote the more comprehensive *Women in Air Force Blue: the story of Women in the RAF from 1918* (Stephens, 1989).

7

CIVILIANS

Almost every man, woman and child had a role to play in Britain's war effort, particularly from late 1941 when there began to be acute labour shortages. In particular, men between the ages of 18 and 50 were conscripted and could be directed to the forces or work in industry, or after 1943 to work down the mines as a 'Bevin Boy'.

Women too were conscripted, although this was initially resisted by the authorities and trade unions. Under legislation passed in December 1941 single women between the ages of 20 and 30 had to choose whether to enter the armed forces or work in farming or industry. By December 1943 one in three factory workers was female and they were building planes, tanks, guns and making bullets needed for the war. The age limit was eventually expanded to between 19 and 43 (and 50 for women who had served in the auxiliary services during the First World War).

In the early years of the war there was a surge of volunteers, most notably to join the Home Guard in the dark days of 1940, but also to enlist in the Women's Volunteer Service (WVS) and other bodies. As the war progressed an element of compulsion was introduced. From 1942, for example, conscripts could be assigned to the Home Guard.

The war affected every aspect of life from food and clothes rationing to one's leisure hours. It is remarkable that there were so few protests or campaigns against these restrictions. Apart from grumbling, the most common practice was to buy forbidden or severely restricted goods on the black market.

The administration of the Home Front, as it came to be called, was complex and constantly changing as the war itself changed. It is also remarkably little explored, although of course there are many books, museums and websites devoted to people's experiences.

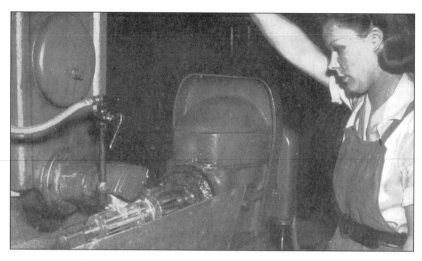

A woman worker concentrating on a lathe. Hundreds of thousands of young women were conscripted to work in factories after 1941. (From Ernest Fairfax, Calling All Arms: the Story of How a Loyal Company of British Men and Women Lived Through Six Historic Years, *Hutchinson, 1945)*

I have highlighted the major sources about individuals, although it should be remembered that most personnel records, where they survive, are still closed to the public, but the individual or their next of kin may be able to obtain copies. If you know where an individual worked, it may be possible to find out where surviving records are held by using the National Register of Archives at Kew or visiting www.nationalarchives.gov.uk/nra. In addition, administrative papers about a person's ration entitlement or service in the Auxiliary Fire Service will almost certainly have long been destroyed

Apart from the official histories relating to the civilian war effort (see Appendix II), the best guide to the records remains John D. Cantwell, *The Second World War: A Guide to Documents in the Public Record Office* (3rd edition, PRO, 1998), although he had academics very much in mind when writing the book, and he rarely looks at sources available elsewhere.

There are a number of websites which look at the how and why (as well as the who), although none are terribly comprehensive. Three I would recommend are:

http://myweb.tiscali.co.uk/homefront/mwindex.html

www.homesweethomefront.co.uk/templates/hshf_frameset_tem.htm
www.jp29.org/2dr.htm.

ALIENS, REFUGEES AND INTERNEES

Hundreds of thousands of foreign nationals were in Britain during the war. Apart from soldiers in Commonwealth and Allied units (see Chapters 8 and 9), there were large numbers of civilians, refugees fleeing from Nazi Europe or citizens from enemy countries who found themselves here at the outbreak of war. The government was naturally concerned that they posed a security threat, so kept a close eye on them. There are a few files in the MI5 papers at TNA in series KV 4-KV 6, with others in Home Office papers, particularly series HO 45, HO 144 and HO 213. Other sources are described in chapter 9.

INTERNEES

Internees primarily consisted of enemy aliens, but during the first two years of the Second World War other aliens were also interned, including refugees who had fled Nazi Germany to escape persecution. By mid-1940, 8,000 internees had been gathered into camps for deportation to the Dominions. This harsh policy was gradually relaxed after the sinking of the SS *Arandora Star* by a U-boat in July 1940, with the loss of 800 lives. Most internees had been released by the end of 1942. Of those that remained, many were repatriated from 1943 onwards. It was not, however, until late 1945 that the last internees were finally released.

The National Archives has many records relating to internment of enemy citizens (usually referred to as aliens). A small sample of 75 personal case files in series HO 214 are particularly useful in depicting the life of an internee. Further files relating to aliens are gradually being transferred from the Home Office in HO 382 and HO 405.

There are index cards in HO 396 for enemy aliens (mostly Germans, Austrians and Italians) interned or considered for internment by Internal Tribunals in 1940. There are two main sets of records: one for those who were exempt from internment and one for those who were interned. The records give family history details such as date and place of birth, address, occupation and details of employers.

Certain information about those men and women where a decision

93

was made to intern may still be closed. In these cases enquirers can request a review of the file by writing to The National Archives (address in Appendix I). Further references to individual internees and internment camps may be found in FO 916. The series consists of general files relating to reports on internment camps and a number of lists of alien internees, arranged by location, name and number of camp.

Nominal lists of internees in camps can be found in HO 215, arranged by name of internment camp; the documents record the internee's name, date of birth and (if applicable) date of release. The series also contains general files relating to internment during the Second World War including subjects such as conditions in camps, visits to camps, classification and segregation of internees, regulations and enactments and the movement of internees abroad. Other Home Office series of records, particularly HO 213, HO 45 and HO 144, also contain a selection of files relating to internment camps.

The Manx National Heritage Library holds much about internment on the Isle of Man, the location of the main camp. Their address is: Manx National Heritage Library, Douglas, Isle of Man IM1 3LY, www.gov.im/mnh.

More details can be found in a TNA research guide, *Internees: First and Second World Wars,* and in Roger Kershaw and Mark Pearsall's *Immigrants and Aliens* (2nd edition, TNA, 2004). A little more information can also be found at www.movinghere.org.uk.

PASSENGER LISTS

Despite the war tens of thousands of civilians (and hundreds of thousands of servicemen) continued to arrive in Britain from outside Europe and the Mediterranean. Their arrival is recorded in passenger lists in series BT 26. It used to be a nightmare finding individual passenger lists, but as the result of an indexing project, they are now easily found by using TNA online catalogue (www.catalogue.nationalarchives.gov.uk). They will tell you the address of individual passengers and their age. Each passenger list was divided into British (and Commonwealth) citizens and Aliens, so if the members of a party were mixed British and, say, American you will need to check both parts of the list. It is rare, however, for individual servicemen to be listed.

Passenger lists for ships leaving British shores to places outside Europe and the Mediterranean are in series BT 27. By the end of 2007, they will be fully indexed and digitised and can be searched at www.1837online.com for a fee.

BEVIN BOYS

In 1943 an acute shortage of coal led young conscripts to be directed down the mines to help boost production. Chosen at random, nearly 48,000 Bevin Boys performed vital but largely unrecognised service, many not being released until years after the war. Ten per cent of all draftees between 18 and 25 were picked for this service.

The Minister of Labour, Ernest Bevin, told the first batch: 'We've reached a point at which there are not enough miners to produce the amount of coal needed to keep the war effort going. We need 720,000 men continuously employed in this industry. This is where you boys come in. Our fighting men will not be able to achieve their purpose unless we get an adequate supply of coal. None of you would funk a fight with the enemy and I do not believe it would be said of any of you boys that you failed to respond to the call for coal upon which victory so much depends.'

Records are held by the Imperial War Museum and by Warwick H. Taylor MBE, Archivist of the Bevin Boys Association, 49a Hogshill St, Beaminster DT8 3AG. The Association is trying to trace all of the nearly 50,000 conscripts who served in the mines. Mr Taylor has also published a booklet on the Boys – *The Forgotten Conscript: A History of the Bevin Boy* (Pentland Press, 1995). There are several websites which provide more information about the Bevin Boys: www.ap.pwp.blueyonder.co.uk/bmd/bevin.htm, www.ewell-probus.org.uk/archive/bevin.htm and www.healeyhero.info/rescue/pictures/reminise/bevin.htm.

CIVIL DEFENCE

Some 60,000 civilians died as the result of enemy air raids. In addition tens of millions of pounds worth of damage was done to homes, factories and offices as well as the infrastructure of the country. Things would have been much worse had it not been for considerable pre-war planning. Some might say, as with the issuing of gas masks and the evacuation of children, there was over-reaction, because the

A clergyman and helpers wander through the rubble after an air raid. (From Ernest Fairfax, Calling All Arms: the Story of How a Loyal Company of British Men and Women Lived Through Six Historic Years, *Hutchinson, 1945)*

authorities over-estimated the potential damage that air raids could do, extrapolated from the damage done to Spanish cities during the Spanish Civil War and the experiences of the First World War. In September 1939 there were 1.5 million men and women working in various aspects of civil defence (of whom 400,000 were volunteers), many of whom drifted off in the long months of the Phoney War.

Despite this, chaos ensued on the outbreak of the Blitz, partly because of rivalry between local government and the various Civil

Defence bodies. A 'freezing order' in July 1940 prevented men in the First Aid and Rescue Parties from seeking other employment. In January 1941 compulsory fire watching was introduced. Both my parents remembered long hours spent on the roofs of the hospitals and how welcome a cup of hot tea was at the end of their shifts. In April 1941 conscripts could be directed to the Civil Defence Reserve, although in practice most members remained unpaid volunteers.

A little more information can be found at http://wearcam.org/decon/cleansing_stations_civildefense.html#cdf.

AIR RAIDS

Extensive records were kept of enemy bombing raids, particularly where bombs fell. Probably the most useful source are the bomb census records and bomb location maps which plotted where every bomb fell and its type. A set of maps are at TNA in series HO 193, with accompanying papers in HO 198. It is possible to find references to raids in London in TNA's online catalogue (www.nationalarchives.gov.uk/catalogue). Outside the metropolis, papers are arranged by location. More about these records can

"Wot? No pets? But 'e won't do nothink in no corners!"

"Alfie, try one of yer 'ackin' coughs—yer father's gorn ter bed wiv the corkscrew in 'is pocket!"

Cartoons by 'Blesbok', a South African cartoonist, on life in communal air raid shelters. (From Reginald Bell, The Bull's Eye, Cassell, 1943)

be found in the TNA research guide *Ministry of Home Security Bomb Census Survey 1940-1945*.

Local authorities kept their own records of bombing incidents. The type of material that you might find includes incident registers, registers of unexploded bombs, fire guard records and log books of air raid warden posts. These documents are now usually at local studies libraries or archives. Another source are local newspapers, although these were often censored to prevent potentially useful information reaching the enemy. Robin Woolven, *The London County Council Bomb Damage Maps 1939-1945* (London Topological Society, 2005) is a facsimile edition of maps kept by London County Council showing where bombs fell on the metropolis.

Raids on towns, particularly the famous ones on cities, such as Coventry and Clydebank, have been written up by local historians, often incorporating the memories of the survivors. Written histories can often be found in local libraries and there are a number of websites devoted to this subject.

CONSCIENTIOUS OBJECTORS

Unlike during the First World War conscientious objectors (COs) were generally tolerated by the authorities and the public. It helped that special conscientious objectors' tribunals, which heard appeals from people who did not wish to serve or in most cases wanted to have their conscription deferred, were generally more sympathetic than their equivalents of the Great War. This ensured that the great injustice which had been done to men of principle of the previous generation was not repeated and, perhaps, more importantly effectively neutered a means of protest against the war.

Of the 59,192 people who claimed conscientious objection (a number four times greater than in the First World War), only 3,577 were given unconditional exemption. Nearly half (28,720) were registered as objectors on condition that they took up approved work, generally in agriculture or civil defence, or remained in their current jobs; 14,700 were registered for non-combatant duties with the armed forces (generally in the Non Combatant Corps); which left 12,200 who had their applications rejected and so remained liable to call up. Only about 4,000 people maintained their opposition to war enough to be imprisoned or court martialled for their beliefs.

There are surprisingly few records about conscientious objectors.

War diaries for the Non Combatant Corps are in series WO 166 at The National Archives. TNA also has a selection of official files about how COs should be dealt with. Small collections of personal papers of individual objectors and organisations, such as the Peace Pledge Union, have been deposited at universities, notably in the Commonwealth Collection at the University of Bradford. An informative article by Juliet Gardiner on conscientious objectors during the war and their fate can be found in November 2004's issue of *History Today*.

FIREMEN

A unified National Fire Service (NFS) only came into existence in August 1941. Before then there were 1,443 local fire brigades, which caused great problems in directing resources to where they were most needed in the big industrial cities during the Blitz.

The National Fire Service reached its peak at the end of 1942, numbering 350,000 in 32 fire forces, each of four divisions, with two columns (100 pumps) per division and a reserve of 20 pumps. A

Many houses in Lake House Road, Wanstead, were destroyed or badly damaged during a raid on 19th March 1941. Fortunately nobody was killed. (From Stanley Tiquet, It Happened Here: The Story of Civil Defence in Wanstead and Woodford 1939-1945, *Borough Council of Wanstead and Woodford, 1948)*

company had ten pumps and a section five. The NFS was controlled by the Home Office but each region had its own Fire Officer, who liaised between the Civil Defence Regional Commissioner and the Fire Force commanders within the region. There were also mobile control units at large incidents. As well as regular professional firemen there were volunteer members of the Auxiliary Fire Service; again, by late 1941 men could be directed to serve in the AFS.

Records of men who served with the London Fire Brigade are with the London Fire and Emergency Planning Authority. They are available to the individuals themselves and next of kin. To get access you need either to email records.services@london-fire.gov.uk or write to London Fire and Emergency Planning Authority, 8 Albert Embankment London, SE1 7SD. Records of men in local brigades may be with the local fire authority or at the appropriate local record office.

IDENTITY AND RATION CARDS

One of the most common documents found amongst a person's papers is their Second World War identity card. They were introduced almost as soon as the war started under the National Registration Act of 1939.

The Act set up a national register containing the names of all citizens, their sex, age, occupation, address, whether they were

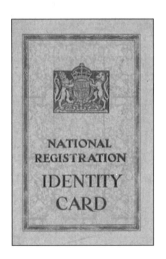

married and whether they had already volunteered for some form of National Service, which census was taken on 29 September 1939. The records still survive (and indeed I have seen them), but they remain closed to the public and are likely to remain so for many years yet.

The data was used by the Government to track the huge numbers of persons who were dislocated due to mass evacuation/essential employment relocation and to provide information essential to implementation of food rationing. Each registrant was issued with an identity card which contained the holder's registration number, full name(s) and current address. Changes of address had to be recorded by the local registrar. All identity card entries had to be verified and certified (stamped) by a registrar. A new set of identity cards was introduced in May 1943. They were finally abolished in February 1952.

The information gathered for ID cards also formed the basis for ration cards. Food rationing was instituted by the Ministry of Food on 8 January 1940. Amounts for basic food items varied from time to time but in mid-war they were typically as follows (per person per week): meat approx. 6 ounces (based on price); one egg (hen or duck); fats (butter, margarine and lard) 4 ounces; cheese 4 ounces; bacon 4 ounces; sugar 8 ounces. Sweets were rationed at 12 ounces per month. Young children and expectant mothers were allowed extra rations including orange juice and cod liver oil. After 1941, tea was rationed at two ounces per week.

In December 1941 a points scheme was introduced to control additional short supply food items such as canned meat and fish, rice, canned fruit, condensed milk, breakfast cereals, etc. Each person was allowed 16 points per month (via designated coupons in the ration book) to be spent for these food items as desired with any retailer who had them in stock, although in practice retailers favoured regular customers. A similar system existed for clothing. Certain items were not rationed, such as beer, bread and cigarettes, but they could be hard to find. Rationing continued until the late 1940s (it was actually at its most severe in 1946 and 1947) when it was gradually relaxed. Meat and bacon finally came 'off-ration' in June 1954.

Although rationing was generally fairly administered and designed to be as nutritious as possible, it was desperately dull and inevitably many people yearned for something special. This desire was met by the black market. Wartime newspapers are full of court reports of ration infringements and people prosecuted for buying or selling on the black market. Heavy penalties were imposed on people, many of whom who would never have considered breaking the law before the war. Ivor Novello went to prison for misusing his petrol ration. The band-leader Victor Silvester was convicted of smuggling because American servicemen helped him to import goods without paying duty. And, ironically, in May 1943, Sir Peter Laurie, Provost-Marshal of the Military Police was convicted at the Old Bailey of rationing offences. For more about these and many other cases see Donald Thomas, *An Underworld at War: Spivs, Deserters, Racketeers and Civilians in the Second World War* (John Murray, 2003).

There are numerous files at The National Archives which are described in John D. Cantwell, *The Second World War: A Guide to Documents in the Public Record Office* (3rd edition, Public Record Office, 1998). Local record offices may have local authority papers relating to rationing and related matters. More information about ID cards and the system used to maintain them can be found at http://myweb.tiscali.co.uk/homefront/natreg/nr.html. There are other websites with pages about rationing and the 'home front' in general, including www.worldwar2exraf.co.uk.

MEDALS

Civil defence workers who served for three years were entitled to the Defence Medal. As with other Second World War campaign medals, they were not issued of right after the war, but had to be claimed. However, it is still possible to claim a medal or seek a replacement. You need to contact the Home Office, 2 Marsham Street, London SW1P 4DF.

The National Archives has a register of cases submitted for consideration of the award of the King's Police and Fire Service Medal for the years 1909-1951 in piece MEPO 22/2.

The George Cross was instituted on 23rd September 1940 to recognise civilian heroism. The Royal Warrant said that the decoration should only be awarded 'for acts of the greatest heroism or of the most conspicuous courage in circumstances of extreme danger'.

The first recipient of a directly awarded George Cross was Thomas Hopper Alderson, an Air Raid Precaution Detachment Leader in Bridlington. Mr Alderson, together with other members of his section, rescued many people trapped under the wreckage of demolished houses. In one incident six people were trapped in a cellar beneath the debris of two five-storey buildings which had been totally demolished. Mr Alderson worked his way into this cellar by tunnelling 13 to 14 feet under the main heap of wreckage and for nearly four hours he worked in a very cramped position, and managed to free all the trapped people. The award of Mr Alderson's George Cross was published in the *London Gazette* on 30th September 1940. The medal was bestowed on over 100 recipients during the war, as well as uniquely to the island of Malta in 1942 in recognition of the collective heroism of the Maltese people.

During the war there were instances when it was not easy to decide whether a Victoria Cross or a George Cross was the more appropriate award. The George Cross and George Medal were intended primarily to reward civilian bravery, but, as many members of the armed forces were unavoidably engaged in work not appropriate for strictly military awards, they became eligible for the GC and GM. Consequently, 78 of the first 100 awards were made to members of the armed forces. The George Cross replaced the Empire Gallantry, Albert and Edward medals and existing holders were invited to exchange their medals for it.

The George Medal was instituted at the same time as the George Cross, and is the second highest award for bravery for a civilian, after the George Cross. Although a lower ranking medal than the George Cross, it has still been very rarely awarded.

Records relating to the George Cross and George Medal are at TNA in pieces WO 373/66-70. Other sources at TNA are described in a research guide *Civilian Gallantry Awards*.

There are several websites which list winners and describe their heroism, particularly the superb www.gc-database.co.uk and www.stephen-stratford.co.uk/george_cross.htm.

A number of books have been written about George Cross and George Medal winners including Ian Bisset, *The George Cross* (MacGibbon & Kee, 1961) and Frederick Carroll, Rose Coombs MBE and Nora Buzzell (eds), *The Register of the George Cross* (This England, 1985).

NATIONAL FARM SURVEY

When the Second World War began in September 1939, Britain was faced with an urgent need to increase home food production, as imports of food and fertilisers were drastically cut. The area of land under cultivation had to be increased significantly. County War Agricultural Executive Committees were set up to increase food production. They could direct what was grown, take possession of land, terminate tenancies, inspect property, and organise mobile groups of farm workers.

One of their first tasks was to organise a ploughing-up campaign under which large expanses of grassland (in some areas land that had not seen the plough since medieval or even prehistoric times) were prepared for cultivation. To assist in this campaign, in June 1940 a farm survey was initiated with the immediate purpose of increasing food production. Between June 1940 and the early months of 1941 some 85% of the agricultural area was surveyed – covering all but the smallest farms.

Once the short-term objective of increasing food production had been met, thought was given to implementing a more general National Farm Survey with a longer-term purpose of providing data that would form the basis of post-war planning. As a source for local and family historians the records of the National Farm Survey are of great value, and for the historical geographer these records present an enormous database of land ownership and land usage in mid-20th century Britain.

The Survey consisted of three components:

- A Primary Farm Record for each farm providing information on conditions of tenure and occupation; and on the natural state of the farm, including its fertility, the adequacy of its equipment and of its water and electricity supplies, the degree of infestation with weeds or pests, and its management.
- A return, taken on 4 June 1941, submitted by the farmer including statistics of crop acreages and livestock numbers and information on rent and length of occupancy.
- A map of the farm showing its boundaries and the fields contained in it.

Every farm and holding of five acres and more was surveyed, including those of market gardeners, horticulturists, and poultry-keepers. The National Farm Survey was begun in the spring of 1941 and largely completed by the end of 1943.

The individual farm records of the National Farm Survey are in series MAF 32 at TNA, with maps in MAF 73. The records are arranged by county and then parish. Similar but less detailed information for Scotland is with the National Archives of Scotland, HM General Register House, Princes Street, Edinburgh EH1 3YY; www.nas.gov.uk.

More information can be found in a TNA research guide *National Farm Surveys of England and Wales, 1940-1943*. The records are also described in Geraldine Beech and Rose Mitchell, *Maps for Family and Local History* (2nd edition, TNA, 2004).

NURSES AND HOSPITALS

Before the Second World War the state played relatively little role in the provision of hospitals and medical services. Hospitals, usually former workhouse infirmaries, were either run by local authorities or were charitable institutions which depended for all or part of their income on donations from local people. During the war this was transformed as the government prepared initially for large numbers of casualties from air raids and then attempted to improve the health of citizens, for example, by providing special wards for expectant mothers.

Records of hospitals are generally either held at local record offices or by the hospitals themselves. Fortunately, there's a detailed online catalogue which tells you which records survive (including records of nurses and patients) and where they can be found, at www.nationalarchives.gov.uk/hospitalrecords.

The National Archives has some registration records of nurses and midwives, all of which are open without restriction. Series DT 10 contains the bound volumes of the Register of Nurses (SRNs). The Roll of Nurses for assistant nurses (later renamed State Enrolled Nurses) which was opened in 1944 is in DT 11. Both male and female assistant nurses, as they were called then, are included on the same Roll, but assistant nurses who worked in mental hospitals were not deemed to be eligible for inclusion. A similar register for midwives is in DV 7. The rolls include: full name, qualifications, where the individual trained, and home address. Any alterations to this information may also be recorded, such as change of name upon marriage, change of address, date of death and any removals from the Register of Roll on disciplinary or other grounds.

More about these records can be found in a TNA research guide, *Civilian Nurses and Nursing Services*.

POLICE

The police force as a symbol of stability and authority took the lead in helping to withstand enemy attacks on the Home Front. Their responsibilities, as well as their symbolic importance as the representatives of an essentially democratic and civilian government (rather than a totalitarian and militaristic one), were enormous. Confidence in the police was vital during this period as, in addition to their normal role of preventing and solving crime, they were responsible for clearing up people's problems arising from the conflict, collecting and cataloguing materials suitable for melting down as weapons of war, and ensuring that the public were issued with gas masks. They also had to work closely with Civil Defence workers during and after air raids, protect key local installations and keep a close eye on foreigners or 'aliens' who could have been spies or saboteurs.

In addition, they had to maintain law and order in towns and cities with limited resources and with their youngest and fittest members away fighting in the armed forces (more than more than two-thirds of the Glamorgan Constabulary, for example, were called up).

Officers could volunteer during the first years of the war, although in the West Riding they were only permitted to do so when volunteering for RAF aircrew duties or as Army Commandos. Service remained a reserved occupation until October 1942 when officers under the age of 25 became 'de-reserved' and liable for services in HM Forces. Increasingly, the constabulary was often staffed only by older officers. To fill this gap the Police War Reserve was set up (including a Women's Auxiliary Police Corps), many retired officers returned to work and men from the reserved occupations were recruited as special constables. Boys between the ages of 14 and 18 were recruited as Police Auxiliary Messengers. Their role was to assist the police with communications by delivering messages on foot or on bicycle.

The organisation of the police service at national level did not change much during the war. Each county maintained its own force and many larger boroughs also had a constabulary. Essex, for example, had a county force and there were small forces in Southend and Colchester.

With the exception of the Metropolitan Police, whose records are at The National Archives (under the MEPO heading), records of local police forces are either at local record offices or still held by the police authorities themselves. A few police forces, such as Glamorgan and Essex, have their own archives, while others maintain museums. They are generally willing to help family historians with their research.

An online memorial to members of the Metropolitan Police who lost their lives in the course of duty (and for those who lost their lives off-duty during air raids) can be found at www.met.police.uk/history/

remembrance.htm. Biographies of the six men from the Essex police forces who lost their lives during the war are at www.essex.police.uk/memorial/ww2.htm.

WOMEN'S LAND ARMY

One popular option for women was to join the Women's Land Army, which was set up in June 1939 to make good the shortage of labour on farms, as agricultural labourers were conscripted. It was not an army in a conventional sense, but a way of assigning young women to work on farms where labour was needed and to ensure that they were properly treated.

A bargee pushes off her narrowboat. Even the near derelict canal system was employed in the war effort. (From V S Pritchett, Transport Goes to War, *HMSO, 1942)*

A passenger hops on a London bus at the height of the Blitz. (From V S Pritchett, Transport Goes to War, *HMSO, 1942)*

At its peak in 1943, there were over 80,000 Land Girls. The women undertook hard farm work including ploughing, turning hay, lifting potatoes, threshing, lambing and poultry management. Some 6,000 women worked in the Timber Corps, felling trees and running sawmills, and over a thousand women were employed as rat-catchers. As the Women's Land Army was not a military force many women did not bother to wear the uniform of green jersey, brown breeches, brown felt hat and khaki overcoat. The Women's Land Army was disbanded in 1950.

The original service records of the Women's Land Army are held by Records Review, Lion House, Willow Burn Trading Estate, Alnwick NE66 2PF. Index cards are available at The National Archives on microfiche in series MAF 421 at Kew. The cards do give a certain amount of information on the individual's service and they cover the period between 1939 and 1948. There are a total of 808 fiche, the final sheet being a compilation of mis-sorts. A small collection of administrative records is held by the Museum of English Rural Life at the University of Reading, Redlands Road Reading RG1 5EX. Some records may be held by local record offices.

There are several histories of the Land Army including Nicola Tyrer, *They Fought in the Fields* (Mandarin Books, 1997) and Joan Mant, *All Muck, No Medals* (Book Guild, 1994). In addition several websites contain short histories of the Army including www.historylearningsite.co.uk/women's_land_army.htm and http://caber.open.ac.uk/schools/stanway/landarmy.html.

8

BRITISH COMMONWEALTH AND EMPIRE FORCES

With the exception of the Irish Free State, which remained neutral throughout what it termed 'The Emergency', the dominions of Australia, Canada, New Zealand and South Africa declared war on Germany in September 1939. Together with India and the British colonies they played a very full part in the war effort. When serving in the European and Mediterranean theatres of war, Commonwealth forces were normally under British command and subsumed for operational purposes into British forces. For example, there were a number of Canadian, Australian and New Zealand squadrons in the RAF. So if you are tracing a Commonwealth serviceman you will probably also need to consult the records described elsewhere in this book.

There was also the semi-autonomous Indian Empire (now India, Pakistan and Bangladesh), which was run by the British under a Viceroy. The Raj was made up of British-controlled India and a number of nominally independent native states, although here the dominant figure was always the British resident. During the war the sub-continent was often in turmoil as politicians such as Nehru, Gandhi and Jinnah pressed for independence. Eventually this was promised in return for support for the war effort. The British Army maintained a number of garrisons in the sub-continent. In addition, there was a separate Indian Army, Air Force and Navy under the control of the Viceroy and commanded by British officers with an increasing number of Indian officers. Indian Army units took part in campaigns in the Middle East, Malaya and Burma.

Lastly, there were dozens of different colonies, some of which had been British since the 17th century. Most were poor and generally contributed little to the Empire, except perhaps occupying a strategic position or supplying raw materials such as rubber or tin for factories in Britain. Colonial men volunteered to serve in local regiments, particularly the King's African Rifles (in East and Central Africa), and the Nigerian and Gold Coast regiments. The African regiments fought in Italian East Africa and Burma.

There are, of course, many books devoted to the actions of particular British Commonwealth forces during the war. However, there is one good general survey by Christopher Sommerville, *Our War: British Commonwealth and Second World War* (Weidenfeld and Nicholson, 1998).

The new British Empire and Commonwealth Museum in Bristol is dedicated to displaying the history of the Empire. It has a large library and museum with a little military material, mainly papers of former colonial officials and regimental magazines. The address is British Empire & Commonwealth Museum, Clock Tower Yard, Temple Meads, Bristol BS1 6QH; www.empiremuseum.co.uk.

COMMON SOURCES

SERVICE RECORDS

Promotions of officers of Commonwealth and Imperial forces are noted in the *London Gazette*. A fully-searchable digital copy of the *Gazette* is available online at www.gazettes-online.co.uk. Promotions, etc also appeared in government gazettes published by the dominions and colonies. The National Archives has an almost complete set of these volumes, to be found within the Colonial and Dominion office records at Kew.

Some records of officers who served alongside the RAF in the RCAF, RAAF, RNZAF or the SAAF are with: PMA(Sec)1b, Building 248A, RAF Innsworth, Gloucester GL3 1EZ. If you are not sure where your man came from, or indeed whether he served in a Commonwealth air force at all, service numbers were prefixed with a number: AUS for Australia; J or C (officers) and R (other ranks) for Canada; and NZ for New Zealand. The South African Air Force had a separate numbering system.

MEDALS

Campaign and gallantry medals were almost identical to those awarded in Britain (see Chapter 2), although the dominions also issued a separate campaign medal to their forces. The awards of gallantry medals to Commonwealth and Imperial forces are noted in the *London Gazette*.

CASUALTIES

Deaths of all Commonwealth forces are recorded on the Commonwealth War Graves Commission online Debt of Honour Register at www.cwgc.org. L. Allison and H. Hayward, *They Shall Not Grow Old* (Commonwealth Air Training Plan Museum, 1991), lists over 18,000 RCAF casualties, together with RAF, RAAF and RNZAF casualties for men who were training in Canada. Records relating to Hindu, Sikh, Muslim, Chinese and Asian merchant seamen who were taken prisoner of war can be found in series BT 373 at Kew.

OPERATIONAL RECORDS

British Commonwealth forces were largely embedded within British command structures, so you may well find unit war diaries, operation record books and other records at Kew, as well as in the country you are researching.

AUSTRALIA

SERVICE RECORDS

The best place to start tracing Australian servicemen and women is the official Nominal Roll, which was created to honour and commemorate the men and women who served in Australia's defence forces and the Merchant Navy. The site contains information from the service records of some one million individuals, although a small number of men and women declined to have their details included. The Roll provides name, rank, service and service number, date and place of birth, date and place of enlistment, date and place of discharge or death. The Roll can be found online at www.ww2roll.gov.au.

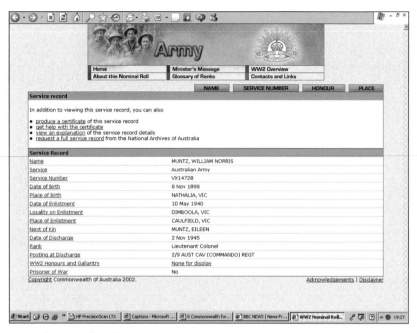

Home	Minister's Message	WW2 Overview
About this Nominal Roll	Glossary of Ranks	Contacts and Links

NAME | SERVICE NUMBER | HONOUR | PLACE

Service record

In addition to viewing this service record, you can also

- produce a certificate of this service record
- get help with the certificate
- view an explanation of the service record details
- request a full service record from the National Archives of Australia

Service Record

Name	MUNTZ, WILLIAM NORRIS
Service	Australian Army
Service Number	VX14728
Date of Birth	8 Nov 1898
Place of Birth	NATHALIA, VIC
Date of Enlistment	10 May 1940
Locality on Enlistment	DIMBOOLA, VIC
Place of Enlistment	CAULFIELD, VIC
Next of Kin	MUNTZ, EILEEN
Date of Discharge	2 Nov 1945
Rank	Lieutenant Colonel
Posting at Discharge	2/9 AUST CAV (COMMANDO) REGT
WW2 Honours and Gallantry	None for display
Prisoner of War	No

Copyright Commonwealth of Australia 2002.   Acknowledgements | Disclaimer

Entry for Lt Col William Muntz on the Australian Nominal Roll maintained by the Australian War Memorial.

A photograph of Lt Col William Muntz of the 9th Australian Divisional Cavalry Regiment in the Middle East. Note the distinctive Sunrise badge on his beret, which has been worn by Australian soldiers since 1914. (From Colin Kerr, Tanks in the East, *Oxford UP, 1945)*

112

An Australian tank crew watch a dogfight over El Alamein, October 1942. From the left, Trooper J.H. Oldham, Lt C.G. Toms, and Sgt S.R. Ferrier. (From Colin Kerr, Tanks in the East, *Oxford UP, 1945)*

Alternatively you can write to The Director, Nominal Rolls, Department of Veterans' Affairs, PO Box 21, Woden ACT 2606.

The Roll is based largely on the service records which are with the National Archives of Australia. You can either consult the file in the reading rooms in Canberra or order copies online. For a charge of $28 (roughly £12) a copy of the whole original record will be provided, for men and women who served in the Army and RAAF, although it is a free service for those who served in the RAN. More details can be found at www.naa.gov.au/the_collection/defence/conflicts/ww2/ ww2.html or write to (for the Army): Central Army Records Office, Department of Defence, GPO Box 393D Melbourne VIC 3001. Or, for the Navy or RAAF, to: Queanbeyan Annex, Russell Offices, Department of Defence, Canberra ACT 2600.

A man's file may include: an attestation (enlistment) form which sets out personal details such as age, next of kin and former occupation; service and casualty forms (B103) recording information about units and postings, injuries and disciplinary charges. There may also be a discharge form that summarises the person's service, a head-and-shoulders photograph of the soldier, along with other documents or correspondence.

Royal Australian Air Force records contain an A3 size 'Personal record of service' form. It sets out personal details such as: age, next of kin, marital status, postings, and training and promotions. The records often contain other material such as enlistment forms, conduct sheets and records of leave. Most also contain a head-and-shoulders photograph of the individual.

The Royal Australian Navy kept 'record of service cards' in the form of double-sided cardboard index cards. They contain personal details such as next of kin, postings, and awards. There are usually one or two cards for each person.

MEDALS

Applications for medals can be made to: Directorate of Honours and Awards T-1-49, Department of Defence, Canberra ACT 2600. More information about medals awarded to Australian forces can be found at www.defence.gov.au/dpe.

CASUALTIES

The Australian War Memorial maintains an online roll of honour at www.awm.gov.au, indicating the unit, date and place of death of the fallen. The information is based on the Roll of Honour displayed at the museum itself. There is also a much smaller Commemorative Roll for civilians who were killed during the war.

OPERATIONAL RECORDS

Records relating to operations undertaken by Australian forces are split between the National Archives of Australia (NAA), the Australian War Memorial (AWM) and, because Australian forces were so closely involved with their British counterparts, The National Archives at Kew (see the appropriate section above).

Among the records at the NAA are: Commando operations; directorates of Military and Naval Intelligence; Women's Royal Australian Army Corps (WRAAC); papers on the loss of HMAS *Sydney* in November 1941; HMAS logbooks; reports of proceedings and ship history files; and RAAF unit records and history sheets.

At the Australian War Memorial can be found: war diaries for 2nd Australian Imperial Force (AIF) and Citizen Militia Forces (CMF) (a number of these war diaries are available online at www.awm.gov.au/database/diaries/index.asp); the papers of the (Australian) Chief of General Staff; and headquarter records of Far East Land Forces (FARELF).

Histories of RAAF units are given in a series of books produced by the RAAF Historical Section, *Units of the Royal Australian Air Force: A Concise History* (10 Vols, Australian Government Publishing Service, 1995).

AUSTRALIAN WAR MEMORIAL

The Australian equivalent to the Imperial War Museum is the Australian War Memorial (AWM), which has a superb collection of research material, and a wonderful museum to visit. An increasing proportion of photographs, drawings and digital images of documents and facsimiles are to be found online: Australian War Memorial, GPO Box 345, Canberra ACT 2601; www.awm.gov.au.

CANADA

SERVICE RECORDS

Service records for Canadian servicemen of the Second World War have not yet been opened. Access is possible only to the files of individuals who died 20 or more years ago. You will need to write, with details of the individual's full name, date of birth and service number (or social security number) to: Personnel Records Unit, Library and Archives Canada, 395 Wellington Street, Ottawa, ON K1A 0N3.

If the individual died after leaving the services, you will also need to prove his or her date of death. Once you have surmounted these bureaucratic hurdles, you should receive a response within a month. More details can be found at www.genealogy.gc.ca/10/100907_e.html.

Brief biographies of air aces are given at www.constable.ca.

MEDALS

Medals and replacement medals can be obtained from the: Honours and Awards Section, Veterans Affairs Canada, 66 Slater Street

Canadian servicemen on sentry duty in Reykjavik during the summer of 1941. Iceland was occupied by British forces in May 1940 in order to protect the sea lanes across the Atlantic. (From Gordon Beckles, Canada Comes to England, *Hodder and Stoughton, 1941)*

Ottawa, ON K1A 0P4. Lists and citations for Canadians in the RCAF and RAF who were awarded gallantry medals, arranged in alphabetical order, can be found at www.airforce.ca/index2.php3?page=honours.

CASUALTIES

There are a number of online resources. For example, the Canadian Virtual War Memorial contains details of the last resting place of 116,000 Canadian and Newfoundland servicemen from all wars of the 20th century (http://www.vac-acc.gc.ca/remembers/sub.cfm?source=collections/virtualmem). There is a digital copy of the hand-drawn and very attractive Book of

A corporal in Canada's famed Princess Patricia's Canadian Light Infantry.
(From Gordon Beckles, Canada Comes to England, *Hodder and Stoughton,*
1941)

Remembrance, containing the names of those who lost their lives, at the same site. The original can be found on Parliament Hill in Ottawa.

OPERATIONAL RECORDS

War diaries, log books and operational record books for Canadian units and ships are with Library and Archives Canada, some of which are listed on the Archives' online catalogue. A very useful site devoted to the Canadian Army in the Second World War is www.mapleleafup.org, with a page on researching men who served in the Canadian forces.

A transcription of the war diary for 1944 and 1945 of the Black Watch of Canada can be found at http://www3.ns.sympatico.ca/laird.niven/public_html/index.htm. The website also includes a database of men from the regiment who lost their lives during this period.

Bomber Command's 6 Group was exclusively made up of Canadian squadrons based in Yorkshire. More about the Group can be found at www.rcaf.com/6group/left.html.

MISCELLANEOUS RESOURCES

Many resources relating to Canada's contribution to the Second World War can be found on the website of the Ministry of Veteran Affairs, www.vac-acc.gc.ca. The Genealogical Centre (www.genealogy.gc.ca), a branch of the Library and Archives Canada, has a number of pages relating to military genealogy and links to other sites of interest. A very informative website devoted to the war brides who came to Canada after the war can be found at www.canadianwarbrides.com/.

INDIA

Records for the Indian Army are largely with the British Library (BL) in London as they inherited the records of the India and Burma Offices after Independence in 1948. Known as the India Office Records (IOR), they now form part of the Asia, Pacific and African Collections. More details are given in Appendix I.

The National Army Museum (again details in Appendix I) may also be able to help, as they have major collections relating to the Indian Army before 1948. The Gurkha Museum, Peninsula Barracks, Romsey Road, Winchester, Hampshire, S023 8TS (www.thegurkhamuseum.co.uk) has material relating to these units.

An Indian unit patrols an Italian hill village. (From The Tiger Triumphs: The Story of Three Great Divisions in Italy, *Government of India, 1946)*

An Indian second lieutenant in Italy. (*From* The Tiger Triumphs: The Story of Three Great Divisions in Italy, *Government of India, 1946)*

An excellent guide to the records in general is Ian A. Baxter, *Baxter's Guide: Biographical Sources in the India Office Records* (3rd edition, Families in British India Society, 2004). Many of the records are described on the Access to Archives (A2A) website, www.a2a.org.uk.

SERVICE RECORDS

Personal files of British officers and warrant officers in the Indian Army (including women's units such as the Women's Auxiliary Army Corps) are in series L/MIL/14 and Royal Indian Navy and Royal Indian Naval Volunteer Reserve in L/MIL/16 at the British Library. Files are opened annually 75 years from the date of entry of the serviceman/woman into the service. Thus records for 1930 were opened in 2006, those for 1931 in 2007 and so on. Other papers and correspondence can be found in series L/MIL/8. Officers are also listed in the *India Army Lists* and the equivalents for other services. The BL has a complete set and incomplete runs may be found elsewhere. Promotions of officers are also given in the *London Gazette*.

The vast majority of ordinary soldiers were Indians (as, increasingly, the officers were as well). Those records are not to be found in London, but where they are is somewhat of a mystery, though the National Archives of India may be able to help. Their address is: Director General of Archives, Janpath, New Delhi 110001; website: www.nationalarchives.nic.in.

After Independence in August 1947, most regiments of the old Indian Army were absorbed into the new Indian and Pakistan armies and are thus still in existence. Some, at least, maintain regimental museums and archives so it may be worth contacting the appropriate unit to see whether they have any material. Brief histories of many regiments can be found at www.regiments.org.

MEDALS AND AWARDS

Gallantry awards are noted in the *London Gazette*.

CASUALTY RECORDS

Casualty returns for officers can be found at L/MIL/14/128-143 at the British Library.

OPERATIONAL RECORDS

War diaries and other records, including some collections of private papers, are held by the National Archives of India in New Delhi. The Imperial War Museum and National Army Museum have published histories and may have other material as well, such as collections of private papers and interviews with veterans. A three-volume set packed with detailed, comprehensive data about every one of the Indian Army's battalions, brigades, and divisions is Chris Kempton, *Loyalty and Honour: The Indian Army, September 1939 - August 1947* (Military Press, 2004).

IRISH FREE STATE

During the war the Irish Free State maintained a benevolent neutrality, but at least 100,000 men served in the British Army and many tens of thousands of men and women found work in factories across Britain. Eire also maintained a small defence force largely equipped with British equipment. Service records for officers (write to Officers' Administration) or other ranks (Other Ranks Administration) can be obtain from Defence Forces HQ, Parkgate, Dublin 8 as appropriate. More information about the activities of the Irish forces during the war can be obtained from the Military Archives, Cathal Brugha Barracks, Rathmines, Dublin 6; www.military.ie/military_archives. Links to various websites devoted to Irish military history can be found at www.regiments.org/nations/europe/ireland.htm.

An entertaining book about Ireland in the Second World War is Tony Gray's *The Lost Years: The Emergency in Ireland 1939-45* (Warner Books, 1997).

NEW ZEALAND

SERVICE RECORDS

Service records for New Zealand personnel are still held by: New Zealand Defence Force, Personnel Archives, Private Bag 905, Upper Hutt. There is no access to service records for personnel still alive. To get access to records of deceased servicemen you will need to prove their death. They do not charge for a single search, but two or more per annum costs NZ$28 (roughly £11). Full details at www.nzdf.mil.nz/personnel-records/index.html. You can also print out a form to request information.

MEDALS AND AWARDS

The Personnel Archives also deal with medal enquiries.

CASUALTY RECORDS

Official information about the location of war graves is held by War Graves, Ministry of Culture and Heritage, PO Box 5364, Wellington. A project to photograph the graves and memorials of all New Zealand servicemen and record the images in an online database can be found at www.nzafmp.org. E.W. Martyn, *For Your Tomorrow* (2 vols, Volplane Press, 1998-1999), provides information on New Zealander casualties in the RNZAF and other air services.

OPERATIONAL RECORDS

Official records of the three services including war diaries and the like, are held by Archives New Zealand, PO Box 12-050, Wellington; www.archives.govt.nz; email: reference@archives.govt.nz.

Unofficial records relating to the New Zealand Army during the war, including unit records, newspapers and personnel papers, are kept by the Army Museum, PO Box 45, Waiouru; www.armymuseum.co.nz. The equivalent for the Royal New Zealand Navy is the Navy Museum, PO Box 32 901, Devonport, Auckland, and for the Royal New Zealand Air Force the Air Force Museum, Private Bag 4739, Christchurch (www.airforcemuseum.co.nz) which maintains a specialist research collection covering the history of the RNZAF and military aviation in general. It includes books and journals; maps and plans; letters, diaries, logbooks and other personal material; photographs; film; and sound recordings.

At the end of the war some 50 official histories recording New Zealand's war effort, including battalion level studies, were prepared. They can now be read online at www.nzetc.org/tm/scholarly/tei-corpus-WH2.html. Names of servicemen and brief biographical descriptions are often to be found within these pages. The Imperial War Museum and British Library in London also has sets. A more approachable introduction is Ian McGibbon, *New Zealand and the Second World War: the People, the Battles, and the Legacy* (Hodder Moa Beckett, 2004), which tells the story of the country's war effort.

MISCELLANEOUS RESOURCES

Pages devoted to New Zealand in the Second World War are at www.nzhistory.net.nz/ww2/index.html. It also has an exhibition gallery devoted to Kiwis in Italy based on a book by Megan Hutching (ed.), *A Fair Sort of Battering: New Zealanders Remember the Italian Campaign* (Harper Collins, 2004). A site devoted to the 3rd Division NZEF, which served in the Pacific, can be found at http://au.geocities.com/third_div, and includes lists of men who served with the Division.

SOUTH AFRICA

SERVICE RECORDS

Service records are held by: Department of Defence Documentation Centre, Private Bag X289, Pretoria 0001. Requests can be emailed to sandfdoc@mweb.co.za. A useful page on researching South Africans who served in the services can be found at www.militarymuseum.co.za/main.htm. Because of the policies of the Union government black South Africans only served in non-combatant roles.

MEDALS

An incomplete set of citations for gallantry awards to South African forces is held by the Military Medal Society of South Africa, 1 Jacqueline Avenue, Northcliff, Johannesburg 2195; email: bickley@global.co.za.

CASUALTIES

The National Museum of Military History (details below) maintains a Roll of Honour for men who fell during the Second World War.

OPERATIONAL RECORDS

Records of the services are held by the Documentation Centre (Department of Defence Archives), Private Bag X289, Pretoria,

0001. It houses the official records of the Department of Defence as well as a collection of unique publications, unit history files, war diaries, photographs, maps and pamphlets pertaining to the Department of Defence and South African National Defence Force. Some other material may be available from the National Archives of South Africa, Private Bag X236, Pretoria 0001; www.national.archives.gov.za.

The South African National Museum of Military History, in a suburb of Johannesburg, has many records relating to the South African war effort as well as displays of artefacts and weapons. Its address is PO Box 52 090, Saxonwold 2132; www. militarymuseum.co.za.

Microfilm copies of SAAF operation record books are at The National Archives at Kew in series AIR 54. Lawrence Isemonger's *The Men who Went to Warsaw* describes in detail all the operations of the men of 31 and 34 Squadrons SAAF during the Second World War, paying particular attention to their supply missions to Warsaw during the Uprising. It is a well illustrated book and has a Roll of Honour, a list of Warsaw sorties and list of the Consolidated Liberator VI aircraft with mention of what happened to them.

THE COLONIES

Because colonial forces and men were regarded as being part of the British armed services, their records and where they can be found are almost exactly the same as for British forces, particularly the Army. For more details see chapter 2 above.

If you are searching for South Asian, Irish or West Indian servicemen it is worth visiting the Moving Here website (www.movinghere.org.uk) which is dedicated to the migration of Jewish, Irish, Caribbean and South Asian people to Britain. Another site devoted to the men from India and the Colonies who served during the war and maintained by the Memorial Gates Trust (www.mgtrust.org) has many pages telling the stories of men from the Caribbean, Africa and the Indian sub-continent who served in colonial, Indian or British forces.

9

ALLIES AND ENEMIES

Researching the war efforts of countries outside the British Commonwealth presents peculiar difficulties. The organisation of forces during the war and the current arrangement of the records may seem baffling. It can be particularly difficult if you are conducting research by post or email, as many archives are not geared up to dealing with researchers. It certainly helps if you can correspond in the language of the country you are interested in. It is also a good idea to do your reading beforehand, and ask questions that can be answered by the archive. In particular, you should know which unit the person you are interested in served with. Although aimed at academics, some sage advice about dealing with the archives of the former Soviet Bloc (and useful addresses) can be found at http://hei.unige.ch/sections/hp/Foreign_archives.htm#selected_foreign.

If access to service records is permitted, it is generally to the veteran him or herself or to the next of kin. Definitions of next of kin vary slightly between archives, but might be taken to be the widow or widower and any children. Sometimes this definition is extended to the brothers, sisters or grandchildren of the veteran. If in doubt you should check with the appropriate archive or agency.

If you are tracing a prisoner of war or civilian internee then the first place to try may be the International Committee of the Red Cross Archive in Geneva, who maintain record cards for the people they helped during the war. Full details are given in Chapter 2.

The Imperial War Museum may well have books that can help your research. It is also worth contacting your local LDS Church family history centre to see whether they can obtain microfilms for you, as the Church has large collections of genealogical material from all over the world. More information about this material can be found at www.familysearch.org. Another useful web resource is Cyndi's List (www.cyndislist.com) which has links to over 250,000 genealogical websites around the world, arranged by country and subject.

BELGIUM

Service records for men who served with Belgian forces are kept by the Musée de 'l'Armée et d'Histoire Militare, Jubelpark 3, 1000 Brussel, www.klm-mra.be (with English pages as well as Dutch and French). A comprehensive website containing histories of Belgian units attached or absorbed into the British Army, Royal Air Force and Royal Navy is at www.belgianbadges4046.be/BE_UK.htm.

CZECHOSLOVAKIA

Almost all service records for Czech service personnel, including the Free Czech forces, are held by the Military History Archive: Vojenský historický archive, Sokolovská 136, 186 00 Praha 8 –

A Czech fighter pilot, a member of 310 Squadron RAF which was comprised of Czech airmen. (From There's Freedom in the Air, *HMSO, 1944)*

127

Karlín. However, records for some Czech airmen who served in the RAF (mainly with the Free Czech 310, 311 and 312 Squadrons) are with: PMA(Sec)1b (2), Building 248A RAF Innsworth, Gloucester GL3 1EZ.

A website containing much about the Free Czech forces is at www.geocities.com/nasenoviny/indexEN.html. Another site devoted to the perils and pitfalls of researching in the Czech Republic is www.shon.150m.com/czechhtm.htm.

Papers of the Czechoslovak Refugee Trust, established by the British Government in 1939, and of its voluntary predecessor, the British Committee for Refugees from Czechoslovakia, are in series HO 294 at Kew. Specimen personal files of refugee families are in pieces HO 294/235-486. Case papers of other refugee families, extracted from files that have not been preserved, are in HO 294/287-611. In many instances these provide a detailed case history.

FRANCE

SERVICE RECORDS

Access to military records is restricted for 120 years from the soldier's birth. They are available only to the veteran or next of kin. However, operational files and some pension papers are now largely open. You will need to contact: Service historique de l'Armée de Terre, Vieux Fort, Chateau de Vincennes, F-94304 Vincennes Cedex; http://jomave.chez.tiscali.fr/adgenweb/shat.html.

MEDALS AND AWARDS

Some French army records, including medal records and pension records, are at: Bureau centrale des Archives Administrives Militaries à Pau, Caserene Bernadotte F-64000 Pau.

CASUALTY RECORDS

Graves and memorials for French servicemen who lost their lives during the war are maintained by the: Ministère des Anciens Combattants et Victimes de Guerre, 139 rue de Bercy, F-75012 Paris.

OPERATIONAL RECORDS

The French Army Museum has extensive galleries devoted to the Second World War and France's part in it: Musée de l'Armée, Hôtel National des Invalides, 129 rue de Grenelle, F-75700 Paris 07 SP; www.invalides.org.

A comprehensive book on the French Army in 1939 and 1940 is Lee Sharps, *The French Army 1939-1940* (2 vols, Military Press, 2002) which provides incredible amounts of data. A simple website devoted to the Free French forces is at http://perso.wanadoo.fr/lepoilu.

GERMANY

SERVICE RECORDS

German service records can be found in one of three different archive repositories, so it is important to know which service a man served with. Austria joined Germany as a result of the *Anschluss* in March 1938, so records for Austrians (and for the nationals of the parts of other countries absorbed into the *Reich*, such as the Sudetenland and Alsace) are to be found in the archives described below.

Most German military service records for the Second World War are held by the Deutsche Dienststelle (WASt) in Berlin. Among their holdings are: an alphabetical Central Registry with over 19,000,000 record cards for Wehrmacht personnel and members of other military/paramilitary organisations; details of postings of individuals between units; 2,100,000 personal files on German naval personnel between 1871 and 1947; more than a million personal documents from members of the Wehrmacht, such as identity cards, pay books, etc; over 15 million files on German and Austrian prisoners of war, mainly in French, American and British custody hands; some 3.1m registrations of deaths; and, miscellaneous files and combined records, such as Army and Air Force List, Honours and Awards, etc

Access is allowed to records of personnel who were killed in action or have been dead for ten years. Records for men presumed missing in action are available 90 years after their birth date. There is a fee of approximately €20: the actual amount depends on how much photocopying is required. The address is: Deutsche Dienststelle

A group of German paratroopers, some of the most feared troops in the early days of the war. (*From Friedrich Frank,* Unser Kampf in Holland, Belgien und Flandern, *Brudmann, 1941*)

(WASt), Eichborndamm 179, D-13403 Berlin. There is a useful website, in German and English, at www.dd-wast.de.

Other records, particularly for the Luftwaffe, the Organisation Todt and the Waffen-SS, are held by the German National Archives (Bundesarchiv) at: Bundesarchiv, Abteigarten 6, D-52076 Aachen; www.bundesarchiv.de/aufgaben_organisation/ abteilungen/zns/index.html. Records are generally opened 30 years after the death of the individual.

Records of members of the Nazi (NSDAP) Party and related bodies (including the SS and SA) were kept by the American-run Berlin Document Center, before they were passed to the Bundesarchiv in 1994. These records are now available at: Bundesarchiv, Abteilung Deutsches Reich, Finckensteinallee 63, D-12205 Berlin, www.bundesarchiv.de/aufgaben_organisation/ abteilungen/reich/00340/index.html.

CASUALTY RECORDS

The German equivalent of the CWGC is the Volksbund

Deutsche Kriegsgräberfürsorge e.V. It can be contacted at: Bundesgeschäftsstelle, Werner-Hilpert-Straße 2, 34112 Kassel; www.volksbund.de.

The website (in German) describes the work of the Volksbund, and contains details of German cemeteries around the world. There is also a searchable database to the war dead, although information is posted to you, rather than directly available online.

A Nazi wound badge in silver, which was given to anyone who had received several wounds or a single serious wound.

OPERATIONAL RECORDS

Operational records of the German Army and Waffen-SS are with the: Federal Archives Military Section, Wiesentalstrasse 10, D-79115 Freiburg-in-Breisgau; www.bundesarchiv.de/aufgaben_organisation/abteilungen/ma/index.html. Unfortunately Luftwaffe records were largely destroyed in the last weeks of the war.

Most German signal traffic was intercepted by codebreakers at Bletchley Park. The raw Ultra Decrypts (as their transcripts were called) are available at The National Archives in Kew in series DEFE 3.

WAR CRIMINALS

The National Archives at Kew has papers related to the war crimes which took place either in the British Zone or by Germans normally resident there. There are card indexes to people they were looking for, or had come forward as witnesses, in WO 353, WO 354 and WO 354, details of trials in WO 325, and papers in WO 309 and WO 311. More information can be found in a TNA Research Guide, *War Crimes of the Second World War*. Yale University has put transcripts of the Nuremburg war crimes and related documents online at www.yale.edu/lawweb/avalon/imt/imt.htm.

Of particular interest are the Consolidated Wanted Lists prepared by the Central Registry of War Criminals and Security Suspects (CROWCASS), which was established by the British and Americans to trace former enemy nationals suspected of committing war crimes or atrocities. These Lists contain over 50,000 names of known war criminals and those suspected of brutality, torture or murder. A set of lists for 1947 are at TNA in series WO 309. They have also recently been published by Naval and Military Press.

THE HOLOCAUST

An estimated 6 million Jews, and many gypsies, homosexuals and disabled people, were killed during the Holocaust, sometimes referred to as the *Shoah* (Hebrew for catastrophy or destruction). The Yad Vashem memorial in Jerusalem is the major repository of information about the Holocaust. It has a library of 100,000 volumes. In addition there is an extensive archive containing primary source material, including many testimonies from survivors. Their library includes over 1,200 *Yizkor* books. These are books which have been published by groups of former residents (generally in Hebrew or Yiddish) as a tribute to their former homes and the people who died during the Holocaust. More about them can be found at www.jewishgen.org/Yizkor, together with links to books which have been translated into English and lists of former residents who perished. The Hall of Names houses the Pages of Testimony (filled out by relatives of Holocaust victims), which is a manuscript collection of information about the victims. There are several million Pages of Testimony and each page contains: names of parents; spouse and children; birth and death dates and places; and details of the person submitting the information. Yad Vashem's address is: Holocaust Martyrs' and Heroes' Remembrance Authority, PO Box 3477, 91034 Jerusalem, Israel; www.yadvashem.org (website in English).

Yad Vashem also maintains a Central Database of Holocaust Victims, an attempt to reconstruct the names and life stories of all the Jews who perished in the Shoah. The database is incomplete and is available online. In the summer of 2004, it was estimated that the number of Jews commemorated in it was close to three million. Millions of names that appear in historical documents have not yet been identified nor recorded in the database; many additional names still linger in the memories of survivors or in the lore of their families.

The database is made up of three basic sources:

- Pages of Testimony: one-page forms, submitted to Yad Vashem by survivors, remaining family members or friends in commemoration of people who perished in the Holocaust. The first 800,000 of them were collected in the 1950s. There are currently some 2,000,000 such pages.
- Historical documentation from the archives, such as the correspondence of the Nazi bureaucrats and their counterparts throughout Europe; personal documents of the Jews such as letters, passports, diaries and memoirs, as well as the documentation of Jewish organs and institutions; lists detailing confiscation of assets, deportations or lists of victims or survivors; legal documentation from proceedings against Nazi criminals and collaborators, and much more.
- Local commemoration projects: there are dozens of local initiatives to record the names of the Jews from a specific region, country, or camp.

There are many research institutes and a profusion of published material is available in central and eastern Europe; however, few institutions are organised for genealogical research. In addition there are few general indexes and much of the relevant published material is not in English.

International Tracing Service (ITS), Große Allee 5-9, 0-34454 Arolsen, Germany was set up by the International Red Cross after the war and maintains 40-million index cards of victims and survivors. It is preferable to direct an inquiry through a national Red Cross committee that will redirect it. Yad Vashem has copies of some of these records on microfilm.

The US Holocaust Memorial Museum in Washington (opened 1993) has a library and archives of Holocaust research material, including documents recently microfilmed in the former Soviet block. They also have a co-operative agreement with Yad Vashem. The Museum can be contacted at: 100 Raoul Wallenberg Place SW, Washington, DC 20024-2150; www.ushmm.org.

The Museum also maintains a Survivors Registry, which seeks to include the names of all Holocaust survivors, facilitates contact between survivors, collects and displays basic information about survivors and assist survivors and their families in their attempts to trace missing relatives. At present there are some 185,000 names in it. A copy is kept at the Holocaust Centre, Beth Shalom, Laxton, Newark NG22 0PA.

Gary Mokotoff's *How to Document Victims and Locate Survivors of the Holocaust: Documenting Victims, Locating Survivors* (Avotaynu Monograph, 1995) is a comprehensive if dated American guide to the subject and the records. There are several websites which provide assistance for anybody researching Holocaust victims or survivors: useful pages can be found at www.movinghere.org.uk/galleries/roots/jewish/holocaust/holocaust.htm and on the website of the Jewish Genealogical Society of Great Britain (www.jgsgb.org.uk). Other (American) sites are http://remember.org and www.jewishgen.org, which has a Holocaust Global Registry page that provides a central place for anyone searching Holocaust survivors, for survivors searching for family members or friends, and for child survivors seeking clues to their identity.

MISCELLANEOUS RESOURCES

An interesting website describing general genealogical research in Germany (in German) with pages devoted to the Second World War is http://wiki.genealogy.net/index.php/Hauptseite. Details of Germans civilians interned in South Africa can be obtained from the Correctional Services Archives, Private Bag X136 Pretoria 0001, South Africa.

ITALY

Service records for Italian forces are held by: Direzione Generale del Personale Militare, 5° Reparto - 15a Divisione, Piazzale della Marina 2, I-00196 Roma. To get access to their records you will need to write to them in Italian. Fortunately a draft letter, and other useful information about researching Italian servicemen and the Italian Navy, can be found at www.regiamarina.it/research.htm. A list of Italian prisoners of war held in South Africa can be obtained from Mr Coccia, PO Box 647, Irene 0062, South Africa.

JAPAN

Many records were destroyed during bombing raids on Tokyo in the last few months of the war. Only records for the Japanese Navy appear to survive. The *Kaigan Shôhei rirekesho* are records of Naval officers and ratings, 1872-1945, including names, dates of birth and death and length of service. These records are with the Ministry of Health and Welfare's Relief Bureau in Tokyo. Records are available only to the families of the deceased.

Junkokusha Meibo is a roll of honour for all of Japan's war dead, which is kept at the Yasukuni Shrine in Tokyo. More details can be found at www.yasukuni.or.jp/English.

The National Institute for Defense Studies has numerous records for both the Army and Navy, including war diaries and naval action reports. More details at www.nids.go.jp/English. Decrypts of intercepted Japanese signals are at The National Archives at Kew in series DEFE 3. The National Archives in Washington has copies of many captured Japanese documents.

The National Archives at Kew has records relating to war criminals, particularly people who were sought for cruelty to former British and Commonwealth service personnel and civilians. Files are in WO 311 and WO 325 with card indexes in WO 356 and WO 357. More information can be found in a TNA Research Guide, *War Crimes of the Second World War*.

NETHERLANDS

Service records for men and women who served in the Dutch armed forces during the war are held by the armed services. For details contact the Defensievoorlichtingscentrum, Postbus 20701, 2500 ES Den Haag, or email defensievoorlichting@mindef.nl. Naval records are held by Directeur Personneel, Koninklijke Marine, Postbus 20702, NL 2500 ES 'S-Gravenhage.

The Dutch War Graves Commission maintains 42 books of remembrance for Dutch citizens who lost their lives during the war and a number of war cemeteries across Europe (including a plot at Paddington Cemetery, Mill Hill in North London) and in Indonesia (formerly the Dutch Indies). Their address is: Oorlogsgravenstichting, Postbus 85981 NL-2508 CR Den Haag; www.ogs.nl.

NORWAY

Operational records of Norwegian forces are kept by: Riksarkivet (National Archives), Postboks 4013, Ullevål Stadion, N-0806 Oslo; www.riksarkivet.no. An informative website devoted to the Norwegian Campaign of 1940 can be found at http://hem.fyristorg.com/robertm/norge. Records relating to war crimes in the country can be found in The National Archives at Kew in series WO 331.

POLAND

Service records for Poles who served in British forces during the war are still held by the Ministry of Defence. For the Royal Navy and Army write to: Army Personnel Centre, Polish Correspondence Section, Kentigern House, 65 Brown Street, Glasgow G2 8EX, and for the RAF: PMA(Sec)1b, Building 248A, RAF Innsworth, Gloucester GL3 1EZ.

Records of the Polish Resettlement Corps, which helped ex-servicemen and women adjust to new lives in Britain in the immediate post-war years, are at The National Archives in series WO 315. There are, however, few references to individuals and a number of records are in Polish.

The Polish Institute and Sikorski Museum at 20 Princes Gate, London, SW7 1PT holds an extensive archive of some 10,000 military items arranged on display in rooms primarily dedicated to the armed forces, many of which served in the Second World War. The Institute archives date back to the 16th century. An extensive library relating to Poland and Poles abroad is kept by the Polish Social and Cultural Association, 238-246 King St, London W6 0RF (www.posk.org). You can email the Library with your query: polish.library@posk.org.

Records of Poles who served in Polish forces are held by the Centralne Archiwum Wojskowe, ul. Poligonowa 2, 00-910 Warszawa Rembertów; www.caw.wp.mil.pl. You will need to write to them in Polish. More information (in English) can be found at http://maxpages.com/poland/Archives_Poland.

An interesting and informative website devoted to the Polish Resistance (Home Army) is at http://polishresistance-ak.org. The history of the Polish RAF squadrons (Nos. 300-309, 315-318, 663) in

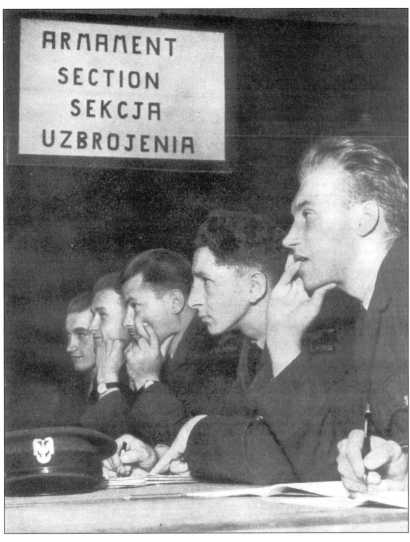

Polish aircraftsmen learn English so that they can service RAF aircraft. (From There's Freedom in the Air, *HMSO, 1944)*

the Second World War is told in: J.B. Cynk, *The Polish Air Force at War: The Official History* (2 vols, Schiffer, 1998).

SOVIET UNION (RUSSIA)

Only now after the end of the Cold War and the admission of Western historians to Russian archives are accurate histories being written (such as those by Anthony Beevor) and the full extent of the suffering endured by the Red Army and other Soviet forces being appreciated.

A Soviet Navy brass belt buckle.

That said, it is extremely difficult to find much about individual servicemen. Service records for officers and men, together with other information about the Russian forces, are held by: Russian State Military Historical Archive 2 Baumanskaya 3, 107864 Moscow.

An excellent English language website devoted to researching

A Red Army tank crew. (From A Polyakov, With a Soviet Unit through the Nazi Lines, *Hutchinson, 1941)*

138

Russian roots is at www.mtu-net.ru/rrr, although it says little about military history.

UNITED STATES

Debra Johnson Knox, *World War II Military Records: A Family Historian's Guide* (Mie Publishing, 2003) is a straightforward, specialised genealogy guide to finding and interpreting key information from military personnel records, casualty reports, WW II draft registrations, burial sites, awards and medals, and more. More details are given at: www.ipgbook.com/showbook.cfm?bookid=1877639915.

SERVICE RECORDS

Unfortunately, some 80 per cent of service records for soldiers and airmen (both officers and enlisted men) were destroyed in a disastrous fire in 1973, although records for naval personnel survive. Surviving material is held by: National Personnel Record Center, Military Personnel Records, Attention: Army Reference Branch *(or Air Force, Navy as appropriate)*, 9700 Page Avenue, St Louis MO, 63132-5100; www.archives.gov/facilities/mo/st_louis/military_personnel_records.html.

To see an individual's records you will need to write to the Center enclosing the appropriate form, which can be downloaded from their website. Veterans and next of kin have full access to their records, other researchers need signed permission from the individual or their family. An article on the workings of the Centre appeared in the Spring 2005 issue of *Prologue*, which can be read at www.archives.gov/publications/prologue/2005/spring/spotlight_nprc.html.

It is likely that files for the Second World War will be opened around the year 2010. Indeed, personnel files for a small number of eminent or famous men have already been released.

MEDALS

Replacement medals for the Army can be requested from the National Personnel Records Center in St Louis, or for the Navy and Marines the Bureau of Naval Personnel, Liaison Office, Room 5409, 9700

Page Avenue, St. Louis, MO 63132-5100. A list of Medal of Honor recipients with citations can be found at www.army.mil/cmh-pg/mohiia1.htm. The Medal is America's most prestigious gallantry medal.

CASUALTY RECORDS

The impressive World War II Memorial in Washington DC honours the 16 million men and women who served in the American armed forces, the more than 400,000 who died, and all who supported the war effort from home. The website (www.wwiimemorial.com) also maintains a Registry of Remembrances, listing Americans who contributed to the war effort. Any US citizen who was involved in the war effort, whether a veteran or someone on the home front, is eligible for inclusion on the Registry.

The website also includes four distinct databases that can be searched for names: those who are buried in the American Battle

Examining the wreckage after the Allied evacuation from Dunkirk. (From Friedrich Frank, Unser Kampf in Holland, Belgien und Flandern, *Brudmann, 1941)*

Monuments Commission's (ABMC) overseas military cemeteries or commemorated on the Commission's Tablets of the Missing; those listed on official War and Navy department's Killed in Service records now at the US National Archives; or, those honoured by public enrolment in the Registry of Remembrances. The information includes service number, service and where appropriate, details of service or where the individual is buried or commemorated. The records are arranged by state. You can also write to the American Battlefields Monuments Commission, Courthouse Plaza II, Suite 500, 2300 Clarendon Boulevard, Arlington, VA 22201 for copies.

There is a Reference Information Paper (no 82), *A Finding Aid to Records Relating to Personal Participation in World War II: American Military Casualties and Burials*, which describes records at the National Archives in Washington. It can be read at http://www.archives.gov/publications/reference_information_papers.

Missing Air Crew Reports (MACR) were compiled after the loss of aircraft or the death of individual aircrew by USAAF Units. Microfilm copies are held by the National Archives and they can be seen at their College Park branch or ordered for a nominal fee by writing to NARA/NNR2, 8601 Adelphi Road, College Park, MD 20740-6001. More information about these Reports is at: www.airforcehistory.hq.af.mil/faq/MACR.htm and an index to them at www.armyairforces.com/dbmacr.asp.

The National Archives and Records Administration (NARA) maintains an online database to prisoners of war at http://aad.archives.gov/aad/series_description.jsp?series_id=644&coll_id=null. It is based on a database compiled at the time and includes information about US military officers and soldiers, and American and some Allied civilians who were prisoners of war and internees. The record for each prisoner provides serial number, personal name, branch of service or civilian status, grade, date reported, race, state of residence, type of organisation, parent unit number and type, place of capture (theatre of war), source of report, status, detaining power, and prisoner of war or civilian internee camp code.

OPERATIONAL RECORDS

The National Archives (700 Pennsylvania Avenue, Washington DC, 20408; www.archives.gov) has many records relating to the conduct and direction of the war, both for the services and civilian agencies.

There are various online leaflets which indicate their holdings, the most comprehensive of which can be found at: http://www.archives.gov/research_room/research_topics. You can also order a free copy by ringing (from the UK) 00-1- 202-501-5235. There is a also a two-volume book describing their collections: Timothy P. Mulligan, *Guide to Records Relating to U.S. Military Participation in World War II* (NARA, 1996, 1998).

The Library of Congress is undertaking a research project recording the memories of veterans. Details, together with a database of people interviewed and sample tapes, can be found at www.loc.gov/vets.

US Army – Unit histories for US Army Units are with NARA, but do not yet appear to be open to public access. You will need to write to the Textual Reference Branch, National Archives and Records Administration, 8601 Adelphi Road, College Park, MD 20740-6001 for more information. Research into the US army is undertaken by the Center for Military History – www.army.mil/cmh – and they may be able to help further.

United States Army Air Force – Unit histories for the Army Air Force are held by the Air Force Historical Research Agency, 600 Chennault Circle, Maxwell AFB, AL 36112-6424. Another useful source for researchers studying the USAAF is the Air Force Historical Studies Office, which maintains a website at www.airforcehistory.hq.af.mil, or you can write for information to 1190 Air Force, Pentagon, Washington, DC 20330-1190. They will also answer simple questions by email (afhso.research@pentagon.af.mil). Two useful sites on the Army Air Force are www.armyairforces.com and, for biographies of air aces (that is, pilots who shot down five or more enemy aircraft), www.acepilots.com.

US Navy – Logbooks for naval ships are with the Modern Military Branch, National Archives, 8601 Adelphi Road, College Park MD 20740-6001. They are all open to the public, but as with their British equivalents generally only include navigational and meteorological details. More information about the US Navy during the war can be found by contacting the Naval Historical Center, 805 Kidder Breese SE, Washington Navy Yard, Washington DC 20374-5060. Of particular importance is the Navy Department Library, which has a huge collection of books and records on Naval History. More details at www.history.navy.mil/library.

Appendix I

LIST OF USEFUL ADDRESSES

Listed below are the addresses (and very brief summaries of their holdings of Second World War material) of archives, museums and other places which you might need to visit in the course of your research.

NATIONAL ARCHIVES AND LIBRARIES

British Library, 96 Euston Rd, London NW1 2DB
tel: 020 7412 7000; www.bl.uk
The British Library is Britain's national library. It has copies of virtually every book published in the UK, together with private papers of statesmen and other important figures. If you are interested in the Indian Army you might need to use the India Office and Oriental Collections (IOOC), which house the records of the former India Office. Catalogues of some of the IOOC material can be found on the Access to Archives website, including lists of British people who joined the Indian Army and Navy. (www.nationalarchives.gov.uk/a2a).

To get access to the Library you will need to apply for a reader's ticket and demonstrate why you need to use the Library's collections. Once upon a time, unless you were a student or academic, it was difficult to gain admission, but the regulations have been considerably relaxed in recent years. There is no need to make an appointment, although you should allow plenty of time to get your ticket.

The library catalogue is available online (http://catalogue.bl.uk). As it includes the vast majority of books published in the British Isles, it is an important resource, especially if you are checking what books have been published about your area or subject of interest.

British Library Newspaper Library, Colindale, London NW9 5HE
tel: 020 7412 7353; www.bl.uk/collections/newspapers.html
The British Library Newspaper Library, which is almost opposite Colindale underground station, houses the UK's largest and most comprehensive collections of newspapers and magazines, some of which were published during the Second World War. A list of their holdings of forces' papers, together with an introductory essay on the subject, can be found at www.bl.uk/collections/warfare2.html. You will need a reader's ticket, although main BL passes are also valid. A catalogue to its holdings is available online. Again there is no need to make an appointment.

Churchill Archive Centre, Churchill College, Cambridge CB3 0DS
tel: 01223 336087; www.chu.cam.ac.uk/archives/home.shtml
The Churchill Archive Centre has the private papers of many of the prominent politicians, military men and scientists of the Second World War period. At its heart is the immense collection of papers relating to the life of Sir Winston Churchill, which are listed in an online catalogue. Indexes to some collections are also to be found at www.nationalarchives.gov.uk/a2a.

Family Records Centre, 1 Myddelton St, London EC1R 1UW
tel: 020-8392 5300; www.familyrecords.gov.uk/frc
The Family Records Centre is a joint venture between The National Archives and the Office for National Statistics. There is no need to make an appointment or acquire a readers' ticket.

On the ground floor you can find indexes to the officers and men who died during the Second World War and order their death certificates (although the information on them probably won't add anything to the information you already have). Certificates cost £7 each (2006 price) provided you have the full GRO reference or, if you do not, you can order them by post for £11.50 from the General Register Office on (0870) 603 7788. You can also order them online, again if you know the full references, at www.gro.gov.uk. These indexes are available online at www.1837online.com (this is a commercial site) or you can buy them on CD from S&N Genealogy (www.genealogysupplies.co.uk; tel: 01722 716121).

You should be warned that the government is proposing to change the civil registration system which may lead to restrictions in obtaining certificates or obtaining certain information to be found on them, although at the time of writing details are very vague.

The indexes for army officers and other ranks indicate the regiment, rank and service number (which could be useful if you want an ancestor's service record). The Marine Death indexes (Royal Navy as well as Merchant Marine) contain the name of the ship and the age of the deceased. A copy is also available on microfilm at The National Archives at Kew. There is also a slim volume of Indian Army deaths, which are largely for officers, showing the unit they served with. Also of interest are chaplains' returns which provide details of births, marriages and deaths at bases in Britain and overseas.

The first floor contains census records. As the latest census available was taken in 1901, these records may not be of much use to you. In any case, the 1901 census (and increasingly the 19th century ones) is available online. Visit www.nationalarchives.gov.uk/census for details. The 1911 census will be opened in January 2012. Perhaps of more use are the extensive collection of databases and access to online resources, including many which otherwise you would have to pay for, to be found here.

Guildhall Library, Aldermanbury; London EC2P 2EJ
Manuscripts Section
tel: 020 7332 1862;
email: manuscripts.guildhall@corpoflondon.gov.uk;
www.history.ac.uk/gh
Printed Books
tel: 020 7332 1868
Prints and Maps
tel: 020 7332 1839;
email: prints&maps@corpoflondon.gov.uk
Guildhall Library in the heart of the City of London is both an archive and a major reference library. Many of the reference books described elsewhere in the text, such as the *Army Lists* and *Lloyd's Register of Shipping,* can be found here. It specialises in records relating to the City and the businesses and people who worked and lived there, although inevitably there is material for much of the rest of country and indeed overseas. Of particular importance is the Lloyd's Marine Collection which contains material about merchant shipping. An

introductory article to the Guildhall Library can be found in issue 108 (September 2004) of *Family History Monthly*.

House of Lords Record Office, House of Lords, London SW1A 0PW
tel: 020 7219 3074; www.parliament.uk
The Record Office holds the archives of Parliament and also has the papers of a number of prominent politicians, including Lord Beaverbrook. A catalogue to their collections can be found online at the Access to Archives website, www.a2a.pro.gov.uk.

Liddle Collection, Special Collections, The Brotherton Library, University of Leeds, Leeds LS2 9JT
tel: 0113 343 5518; www.leeds.ac.uk/library/spcoll/liddle
The Liddle Collection is a major collection of private papers and other material relating to the two world wars. A catalogue of its holdings for the Second World War can be found online.

Liddle Hart Centre for Military Archives, King's College London, Strand, London WC2R 2LS
tel: 020 7848 2187; www.kcl.ac.uk/lhcma
The Centre holds the papers of 500 senior members of the defence forces. They also maintain an online database to the location of papers of senior defence personnel elsewhere in the UK.

The National Archives, Ruskin Ave, Kew, Richmond,
Surrey TW9 4DU
tel: 020 8392 5200; www.nationalarchives.gov.uk
The National Archives (TNA, formerly the Public Record Office) is the national archives of the United Kingdom. It has major collections of material relating to the Second World War, which are fully described both elsewhere in this book and in John D. Cantwell's *The Second World War: a Guide to Records in the Public Record Office* (3rd edition, Public Record Office, 1998). The comprehensive, and easy to use, catalogue to all 9.5m records held by the Archives is online at www.nationalarchives.gov.uk/catalogue. Another useful aid is a series of research guides which can be downloaded from the TNA website (click on the research button on the homepage and follow the links), or you can pick them up in the Research Enquiries Room at Kew or by ringing (or writing to) the Archives. Where appropriate they are mentioned in the text above.

To get access to this material you will need a reader's ticket, which will be issued on your first visit. There is no need to make an appointment, but you will need to bring some form of identity with you. TNA is a huge place and can be very confusing to first-time visitors, although there are tours which can help you find your feet. There are several reading rooms on the first floor for documents, microfilm and microfiche, and (on the second floor) for maps and large documents. Also on the first floor is the Research Enquiries Room (RER) which has numerous catalogues and card indexes, and where you can ask the friendly and knowledgeable staff about your research.

The Archives has a bookshop, with an excellent range of military books, a restaurant and internet workstations. There is also a small museum displaying treasures from TNA's holdings, often including a few items from the Second World War.

Second World War Experience Centre, 5 Feast Field (off Town Street), Horsforth, Leeds LS18 4TJ
tel: 0113 258 9637; www.war-experience.org
The Centre has sizeable collections showing the experiences of ordinary men and women, both in the services and on the 'Home Front' during the war and welcomes the donation of further collections from readers. Extracts from their holdings can be found on their website. Unfortunately they are unable to help individual researchers.

Society of Genealogists, 14 Charterhouse Buildings, Goswell Road, London EC1M 7BA
tel: 020 7251 8799; www.sog.org.uk
The Society's Library provides a major resource for family historians, with much material that may not easily be found elsewhere. Holdings for the Second World War include sizeable collections of regimental histories and Army and Navy Lists, together with other books. They have a good range of CD-ROMs and free access to the large number of databases on the Ancestry.com website. Non-members pay a fee to use the library: the 2006 current rate is £4 per hour or £14 a day.

Wellcome Library for the History and Understanding of Medicine, 210 Euston Road, London NW1 2BE
tel: 020 7611 8722; http://library.wellcome.ac.uk

The Wellcome Library preserves the records of medicine past and present to foster understanding of medicine, its history and its impact in society. It has one of the world's greatest collections of books, manuscripts, pictures and films about the meaning and history of medicine, from the earliest times to the present day. There are some collections relating to the cure of and assistance to sick and wounded servicemen, all of which can be checked by using their online catalogue.

NATIONAL MUSEUMS

Fleet Air Arm Museum, RNAS, Yeovilton , Ilchester BA22 8HT
tel: 01935 840565; www.fleetairarm.com
The Museum has displays about the Fleet Air Arm during the Second World War. In addition the Centre for Naval Aviation Records and Research has records about many individual members of the FAA, squadron line books (roughly equivalent to Operation Record Books), photographs and maps. Staff members are extremely helpful and knowledgeable. However, at present there is a waiting list of around a year before your enquiry can be researched, and in addition a fee may be levied, so it may be best to visit the Museum to conduct your own research.

Imperial War Museum, Lambeth Road, London SE1 6HZ
tel: 020-7416 5000; www.iwm.org.uk
After The National Archives, the Imperial War Museum is the most important source for the Second World War ranging from artefacts to

The Firepower Museum in Woolwich which houses the Royal Artillery Museum archives.

A Spitfire in the Imperial War Museum.

photographs and films, via books and documents. The major departments are Documents (with collections of private papers of all ranks from Private to Field Marshal), Photographs (40,000 images taken by official photographers), and Printed Books (books relating to all aspects of the war in Britain and elsewhere).

Anybody is welcome to use the research collections, although you must book an appointment at least a day in advance. The holdings are described in a free leaflet, *The Collections: an Access Guide*, which can be picked up at the museum or requested by phone, and is also available online. There is an online catalogue to some of the holdings, including considerable amounts of Second World War material, which personally I find very confusing to use. The website includes information about using the Museum for family history.

There are a large number of Second World War-related exhibits to be seen in the Museum, from Japanese one-person submarines to a Spitfire. Perhaps the highlight, if that is the right word, is the chilling Holocaust galleries. There is also an excellent bookshop and an expensive café. There are no research facilities at either the Museum's branches at Duxford or the new IWM North in Manchester.

National Army Museum, Royal Hospital Road, London SW3 4HT
tel: 020 7730 0717; www.national-army-museum.ac.uk
The Museum contains an impressive library with excellent runs of the *Army List* and *London Gazette*. In addition it holds records relating to soldiers' estates. These are of particular value as they frequently contain details of next-of-kin. They also have major collections relating to the Indian Army. Unfortunately, getting access to their reading room is a bureaucratic nightmare. Indexes to some holdings are now on the Access to Archives website (www.nationalarchives.gov.uk/a2a). There is a bookshop and café. They also organise regular lunchtime lectures and conferences, often with a Second World War theme.

National Maritime Museum, Greenwich, London SE10 9NF
tel: 020 8858 4422; www.nmm.ac.uk
The Museum's Library and Archives holds the largest collection of material relating to Britain's maritime history in the world and is particularly useful if you are researching individual merchant or RN ships. The Library's catalogue is online.

RAF Museum, Graham Park Way, London NW9 5LL
tel: 020 8205 2266; www.rafmuseum.org.uk
The Museum's Library and Archives have substantial holdings about the history of aviation and the RAF in particular. You can use the Archives to trace the history of individual aircraft, for example through the Aircraft Movement Cards (Form 78) and Aircraft Crash Cards and related records. There are also extensive collections of private papers, photographs and building and site plans for RAF stations and airfields. The Library has an extensive collection of Air Publications, navigation maps and books on all aspects of aviation. They also publish a series of excellent information sheets on personnel records, and station, unit and aircraft service histories, which can be downloaded from their website (www.rafmuseum.org.uk/london/research/enquiries.cfm) or requested by ringing the Museum.

Royal Marines Museum, Eastney Barracks, Southsea, PO4 9PX
tel: 01705 819385; www.royalmarinesmuseum.co.uk
Has extensive holdings about the Royal Marines, including a world class library and a large photographic collection.

Royal Naval Museum, HM Naval Base (PP66), Portsmouth PO1 3NH
tel: 023 9272 7562; www.royalnavalmuseum.org
Has large manuscript and library collections relating to the Royal
Navy including material for the Second World War. There is also a
substantial oral history archive of interviews with former sailors and
22,000 images of war ships. Details of the most significant collections
are listed at www.nationalarchives.gov.uk/nra. A charge, at the time
of writing £10, is made for research conducted by staff which lasts
more than half an hour.

Regimental museums

Almost every Army regiment and corps has a museum, which displays
its history and regimental memorabilia such as the silver used in the
officers' mess or items captured from the enemy. Attached to these
museums are often regimental record offices, which may have records
about individual officers or soldiers, collections of photographs and
printed ephemera including regimental journals. However, what they
have varies dramatically. The Essex Regiment Museum, for example,
has almost no official records, although they have a useful database of
material built up over many years about individuals who served with
the regiment. All regimental museums, addresses and opening hours
are given in Terence and Shirley Wise, *A Guide to Military Museums
and Other Places of Military Interest* (10th edition, Terence Wise,
2001). Similar information can be found on the web at
www.armymuseums.org.uk.

Neither the Navy nor the RAF has such a range of local museums.
The major Naval museums are listed above. There are a number of
local air museums, often based at old RAF stations, many of which
have archives about the base, the men who served there and the
aircraft they are trying to preserve. Lists of such museums can be
found at www.museum-explorer.org.uk and www.thunder-and-
lightnings.co.uk/links/museums.html. Details are also given in the
Wises' book, above.

SOCIETIES

Unlike for the First World War, there is no research society dedicated
to the war as a whole. However there are many dozens of societies and
groups which look at aspects of the war. Most societies have websites,
so it is worth surfing the internet to see what is available. In addition

most of the museums listed above and elsewhere in the text have friends' organisations which may be worth joining.

There are two national organisations worthy of your notice:

War Memorials Trust, 4 Lower Belgrave Street, London SW1W 0LA
www.war-memorials.com
Formerly known as Friends of War Memorials, the Trust exists to protect and preserve war memorials and to educate the public as to their value and importance.

Royal British Legion, 48 Pall Mall, London SW1Y 5JY
tel: 0845 772 5725; www.britishlegion.org.uk
Britain's leading charity providing financial, social and emotional support to millions who have served and are currently serving in the Armed Forces, and their dependants. Currently, nearly 11 million people are eligible for their support and they receive around 300,000 calls for help every year. They are of course famous for the annual poppy appeal. There is also a network of local British Legion social clubs for ex-servicemen and women.

Appendix II

BIBLIOGRAPHY

✣

With the possible exception of the American Civil War, no conflict has ever been written about more. Even 60 years after its end, hundreds of books on the Second World War are still published each year, most of which are extremely technical. If you want to know what is still being published visit this website: www.sonic.net/%7Ebstone/index.shtml, which is dedicated to new books about the war.

We include a selection of books here which are likely to be those most useful in your research or which provide an introduction to the war. It is very much a personal choice.

There is an online bibliography to military titles at www.armymuseums.org.uk, although it is by no means complete. The British Library Integrated Catalogue includes almost every book published in Britain, which can be checked at http://catalogue.bl.uk. The Imperial War Museum has reading lists to various topics which can be useful introductions (http://collections.iwm.org.uk/server/show/nav.00g006002).

To see which books are currently in print, visit the Amazon Books site (www.amazon.co.uk), which also includes links to many second hand booksellers. Another similar site is www.historydirect.co.uk. Amazon often offers very good deals on bestsellers, but you should look out for high postage and packing charges. However, your local bookshop should be able to get any book in print for you within a few days.

GENERAL REFERENCE BOOKS

Janet Foster and Julia Sheppard, *British Archives: A Guide to Archive Resources in the United Kingdom* (4th edition, Macmillan, 2001)

Jeremy Gibson and Pamela Peskett, *Record Offices and How to Find Them* (8th edition, Federation of Family History Societies, 2002)
Terence and Shirley Wise, *A Guide to Military Museums and Other Places of Military Interest* (10th edition, Terence Wise, 2001)

FAMILY HISTORY REFERENCE BOOKS

David Annal, *Easy Family History* (TNA, 2005)
Simon Fowler, *The Joy of Family History* (PRO Publications, 2001)
Mark Herber, *Ancestral Trails: The Complete Guide to British Family History and Genealogy* (2nd edition, Sutton Publishing, 2004)
Stuart Raymond, *An Introduction to Family History* (Federation of Family History Societies, 2006)
Christina K. Schaffer, *The Great War: A Guide to the World's Fighting Men and Volunteers* (Genealogical Publishing Company, 1998) – also contains details of archives and records pertinent to the Second World War

OFFICIAL HISTORIES

After the war the government commissioned teams of historians to prepare detailed official histories of the war, formally known as the *History of the Second World War: United Kingdom Military Series* (there is also a civilian series). In announcing their commissioning, the then prime minister Clement Attlee told the House of Commons in November 1946, that their purpose was 'to provide a broad survey of events from an inter-service point of view rather than separate accounts of the parts played by each of the three services'. The main series are: *Grand Strategy* (6 vols); *The Defence of the United Kingdom*; *The War in France and Flanders 1939-1940*; *Victory in the West* (2 vols); *The War against Japan* (5 vols); *The Mediterranean and Middle East* (6 vols); *The War at Sea 1939-1945* (3 vols); *The Strategic Air Offensive* (4 vols); and *British Intelligence in the Second World War* (5 vols).

Commonwealth countries (and the USA) produced similar analyses of their war effort. Those for New Zealand are available online at www.nzetc.org/corpora/WH2.htm.

Because of their specialist nature they tend to be hard going for the novice, although they are essential for understanding how a unit's activities fitted into the bigger picture. The IWM and The National Archives have complete sets. Other libraries may have incomplete sets. The IWM and the Naval and Military Press publish reprints of many volumes.

In addition most regiments and corps have published semi-official histories outlining their activities during the war. The most complete set of these histories is held by the Imperial War Museum, although the Society of Genealogists also has a good collection. Local libraries are likely to have volumes for local units. A number of volumes have been reprinted by Naval and Military Press.

Two bibliographies of regimental histories are Roger Perkins, *Regiments: Regiments and Corps of the British Empire and Commonwealth 1758-1993: a Critical Bibliography of their Published Histories* (David and Charles, 1994) and Arthur S. White, *A Bibliography of Regimental Histories of the British Army* (London, Stamp Exchange, 1988). Both volumes have been published on CD as *Armies of the Crown* (Naval and Military Press).

GENERAL HISTORIES AND ACCOUNTS

Richard J. Aldrich, *Witness to War: Diaries of the Second World War in Europe and the Middle East* (Doubleday, 2004)
Max Arthur, *Forgotten Voices* (Ebury Press, 2004)
Peter Calvocoressi (ed), *The Penguin Book of the Second World War* (Penguin, 2001)
Ian Dear (ed), *The Oxford Companion to the Second World War* (Oxford UP, 2001)
John Ellis, *The World War II Databook* (Aurum Press, 1993)
Martin Gilbert, *Second World War* (Weidenfeld and Nicolson, 1989)
Richard Holmes, *Battlefields of the Second World War* (BBC Books, 2001)
John Keegan, *Second World War* (Pimlico, 1997)

Almost every book by Antony Beevor, Martin Gilbert, Richard Holmes, Max Hastings, or Martin Middlebrook is well worth reading.

ARMY

REFERENCE

George Forty, *The British Army Handbook 1939-1945* (Sutton Publishing, 2002)

Simon Fowler, *Tracing your Army Ancestors* (Pen and Sword, 2006)

Imperial War Museum, *Tracing your Family History: Army* (IWM, 2000)

William Spencer and Simon Fowler, *Army Records for Family History* (PRO Publications, 1998)

GENERAL

Michael Carver, *Britain's Army in the Twentieth Century* (Macmillan, 1998)

David Fraser, *And We Shall Shock Them: The British Army in the Second World War* (Cassell, 1999)

Richard Holmes, *Imperial War Museum: The D-Day Experience from the Invasion to the Liberation of Paris* (Carlton, 2004)

Julian Thompson, *Imperial War Museum's Victory in Europe Experience: From D-Day to the Destruction of the Third Reich* (Carlton, 2005)

ROYAL NAVY

REFERENCE

K.V. Burns, *Badges and Battle Honours of HM Ships* (Maritime Books, 1986)

J.J. Colledge and Ben Warlow, *Ships of the Royal Navy: The Complete Record of All Fighting Ships of the Royal Navy from the Fifteenth Century to the Present* (Greenhill Books, 2003)

IWM, *Tracing Your Family History: Royal Navy* (Imperial War Museum, 1999)

Bruno Pappalardo, *Tracing Your Naval Ancestors* (PRO Publications, 2003)

John M. Young, *Britain's Sea War: A Diary of Ship Losses, 1939–1945* (Patrick Stephens, 1989)

GENERAL

Richard Hough, *The Longest Battle: The War at Sea, 1939-1945* (Cassell, 2003) is a general introduction to the naval campaigns of the Second World War.

Christopher McKee, *Sober Men and True: Sailors' Lives in the Royal Navy 1900-1945* (Harvard UP, 2003)

Julian Thompson, *The Imperial War Museum Book of the War at Sea* (Sidgwick and Jackson, 1997)

ROYAL AIR FORCE

REFERENCE

Philip Congdon, *Per Ardua Ad Astra: A Handbook of the Royal Air Force* (Airlife, 1987)

Ken Delve, *The Source Book of the RAF* (Airlife, 1994)

Simon Fowler et al, *RAF Records in the PRO* (Public Record Office, 1994)

Malcolm Hobart, *Badges and Uniforms of the Royal Air Force* (Pen and Sword Books, 2000)

Imperial War Museum, *Tracing Your Family History: Royal Air Force* (IWM, 2000)

Philip Moyes, *Bomber Squadrons of the RAF and Their Aircraft* (Macdonald, 1976)

John Rawlings, *Fighter Squadrons of the RAF and Their Aircraft* (Crécy Publishing, 1993)

William Spencer, *Air Force Records for Family Historians* (PRO Publications, 2002)

GENERAL

Chaz Bowyer, *The Royal Air Force 1939-1945* (Pen & Sword Paperbacks, 1996)

Max Hastings, *Bomber Command* (Michael Joseph, 1980)

There are also several online bibliographies for the RAF:

www.rafweb.org/bibliography.htm (lists of books on RAF stations, organisation etc)

www.raf.mod.uk/history/ww2ops_bib.html#ww2_bib (AHB general bibliography)

MERCHANT NAVY

REFERENCE

Imperial War Museum, *Tracing Your Family History: Merchant Navy* (IWM, 2000)

Kelvin Smith et al, *Records of Merchant Shipping and Seamen* (PRO Publications, 1998)

Chris Watts, *My Ancestor was a Merchant Seaman* (2nd edition, Society of Genealogists, 2002)

GENERAL

Bernard Edwards, *The Quiet Heroes: British Merchant Seamen at War* (Leo Cooper, 2002)

Peter Elphick, *Lifeline: The Merchant Navy at War, 1939-45* (Chatham Press, 2003)

Martin Middlebrook, *Convoy: The Greatest U-Boat Battle of the War* (Cassell, 2003)

Richard Woodman, *Arctic Convoys: 1941-1945* (John Murray, 2004)

THE HOME FRONT

GENERAL

Corelli Barnett, *The Audit of War: The Illusion and Reality of Britain as a Great Nation* (Macmillan, 1986)

Angus Calder, *The People's War: Britain 1939-1945* (Pimlico, 1992)

Juliet Gardiner, *Wartime: Britain 1939-1945* (Headline, 2004)

Norman Longmate, *How We Lived Then: A History of Everyday Life during the Second World War* (Pimlico, 2002)

Maureen Waller, *London 1945: Life in the Debris of War* (John Murray, 2004)

MAGAZINES

There are several magazines devoted to military history which regularly include articles about the Second World War, notably *The Second World War Magazine*, which is published by Great Northern Publishing, PO Box 202, Scarborough YO11 3GE (http://

www.greatnorthernpublishing.co.uk/the-second-world-war.htm).

Family and general history magazines also regularly publish relevant articles, certainly *Ancestors* (which I edit) does. Find out more at www.ancestorsmagazine.co.uk.

BOOK PUBLISHERS

Publishers of military books about the Second World War include:

Naval & Military Press, Unit 10, Ridgewood Industrial Park, Uckfield TN22 5QE; www.naval-military-press.com. They have an active publishing programme of CD-ROMs and reprints of official publications and official histories. They also sell books relating to warfare, which are described in regular catalogues sent to subscribers. It is worth subscribing as the catalogues provide a reasonable guide to what is in print and often offer books at a discounted price.

Pen & Sword Books Ltd, 47 Church St, Barnsley S70 2AS; www.pen-and-sword.co.uk. They publish books under their own and the Leo Cooper imprint.

Sutton Publishing, Phoenix Mill, Thrupp, Stroud GL5 2BU; www.suttonpublishing.co.uk.

Appendix III

CODENAMES AND ABBREVIATIONS

CODENAMES

Almost all operations, whether Allied or Axis, were assigned codenames to preserve secrecy, and will often be described as such in official papers of the period. Here are a selection of the most important. Traditionally, operation names were written in capital letters:

ANVIL	Allied invasion of Southern France, August 1944 (also DRAGOON)
ARGONAUT	Yalta Conference, February 1945
AVALANCHE	Allied attack on Narvik, May 1940
AVONMOUTH	Allied invasion of Salerno, September 1943
BARBAROSSA	Invasion of Russia, June 1941 (German)
BOLERO	Build up of American forces in Britain before D-Day
CAPITAL	British invasion of Northern Burma, 1944
CHASTISE	Dambusters Raid, May 1943
CIRCUS	Random attacks on German units, trains etc by British fighter bombers, 1943-1945
COCKADE	Allied deception operations prior to D-Day
CRUSADER	The break out from El Alamein
DYNAMO	Withdrawal from France at Dunkirk, May-June 1940
HUSKY	Allied invasion of Sicily, July 1943
JUBILEE	Raid on Dieppe, August 1942
JUNO	D-Day beach

LIGHTFOOT	The Battle of El Alamein
MARKET GARDEN	The operation to capture Arnhem, September 1944
MILLENNIUM	1,000 bomber raid on Cologne, April 1942
NEPTUNE	Naval part of Operation Overlord
NOBALL	Allied bombing raids on V1 and V2 launch sites, 1944
OBOE	British airborne navigational device
OLIVE	Allied assault on Gothic Line in Italy, August 1944
OMAHA	D-Day beach
OVERLORD	D-Day landings, June 1944
PEDESTAL	Relief convoy to Malta, August 1942
PLUNDER	Anglo-Canadian crossing of the Rhine, March 1945
POINTBLACK	Allied strategic bombing offensive against Germany from 1943
PRICELESS	Allied operations in the Mediterranean, 1943
RING	Soviet assault at Stalingrad, January 1943
SEELÖWE (sealion)	Planned invasion of Britain, Autumn 1940 (German)
SHINGLE	Allied landings at Anzio
SWORD	D-Day beach
TAIFUN (Typhoon)	German push towards Moscow, September 1941
TERMINAL	Allied conference at Potsdam, July 1945
THUNDERCLAP	British Air Raid on Dresden, February 1945
TORCH	American landings in Morocco and Algeria, November 1942
TUBE ALLOYS	Euphemism used for the development of the atom bomb
UTAH	D-Day beach
VARSITY	Allied airborne landings across the Rhine, March 1945
WINDOW	Metallic chaff dropped by British bombers to confuse German radar-directed fighters.

Source: www.secondworldwar.co.uk

ABBREVIATIONS

Military documents are full of abbreviations. A list of common ones is given below:

AA	anti-aircraft

AAA	anti-aircraft artillery
AAC	Army Air Corps
AAEE	Aeroplane and Armament Experimental Establishment
AAF	Army Air Force (US), Auxiliary Air Force (UK)
ab or a/b	airborne
ac	aircraftsman
ac or a/c	aircraft
AC or A/Cdr	Air Commodore
ACM	Air Chief Marshal
ACSEA	Air Command South East Asia
ADGB	Air Defence of Great Britain (successor to Fighter Command)
ADRU	Aircraft Delivery and Reception Unit
AEAF	Allied Expeditionary Air Force
AFS	Advanced Flying School, Auxiliary Fire Service
ag or a/g	air gunner
AHB	Air Historical Branch
AI	aircraft interception, air interpretation, air intelligence
AM	air marshal, air ministry, air mechanic
amn	ammunition
AMWO	Air Ministry Weekly Order
armd	armoured
ARV	Armoured Recovery Vehicle
aslt	assault
ATA	Air Transport Auxiliary
ATAF	Allied Tactical Air Force
ATC	Air Training Corps, Air Traffic Control
ATFERO	Atlantic Ferry Organisation
ATU	Aircrew Training Unit
AVM	Air Vice Marshal
BAFO(G)	British Air Forces of Occupation (Germany)
BBRM	British Bombing Research Mission
BBSU	British Bombing Survey Unit
BC	Bomber Command
BCATP	British Commonwealth Air Training Plan
bde	brigade
bdr	bombardier
BEF	British Expeditionary Force
bn	battalion

brig	brigadier
bty	battery
capt, cpt	captain
CAS	Chief of the Air Staff
CC	Coastal Command
CD	Civil Defence
cdo	commando
cdr	commander, commodore
CFS	Central Flying School
CH	chain home (radar station)
CIU	Central Interpretation Unit
CO	commanding officer
col	colonel
comms	communications
COS	chiefs of staff
coy	company
CP	command post
cpl	corporal
CTZ	control zone
CU	conversion unit
CWS	Central Wireless School
D	deputy, director
DBR	damaged beyond repair (aircraft)
def	defence, defended, etc
dep	depot
det	detachment, detach
div	division
dmr	drummer
DZ	drop(ping) zone
e/a	enemy aircraft
EANF	Empire Air Navigation Flight
ech	echelon
EFS	Empire Flying School
emb	embark
en	enemy
engr	engineer
Ex	Exercise
estb	establish
ETA	estimated time of arrival
ETD	estimated time of departure

ETO	European Theatre of Operations (US)
F/Lt	flight lieutenant
f/s or f/sgt	flight sergeant
FAA	Fleet Air Arm
FC	Ferry Command, Fighter Command
FEAF	Far East Air Force
FIDO	Fog Investigation and Disposal Operations
fl o or fl/o	flight office
flt	flight
flt/cdr	flight commander
FM	field marshal
fmn	formation
FOO	forward observation officer (artillery)
fwd	forward
G/C, G/Cpt	Group Captain
GAF	German Air Force (ie Luftwaffe)
gd	guard
gen	general
GHQ	General Headquarters
gnr	gunner
gp	group
GPR	Glider Pilot Regiment
GS	General Staff
gsm	guardsman
hc	high capacity (bomb)
HE	high explosive
HG	Home Guard
HP	high power
HQ	headquarters
hy	Heavy
i/c	in charge, intercom
IAF	Indian Air Force
IB	incendiary bomb
IFF	identification friend or foe
indep	independent
inf	infantry
int	intelligence
IO	intelligence officer
KAR	King's African Rifles
KIA	killed in action

kt	knot (speed)
LAC	Leading Aircraftsman
LACW	Leading Aircraftwoman
LCI	landing craft infantry
LCpl / L / Cpl	lance corporal
LCT	landing craft tank
ldr	leader
LO	Liaison officer
LofC	lines of communication
LSU	Lancaster Servicing Unit
Lt	Lieutenant
lt	light
MAAF	Mediterranean Allied Air Force
maj	Major
MB	motorboat
MC	medium capacity (bomb)
Mc, M / c	motorcycle
ME	Middle East
med	medium, medical
MFH	mobile field hospital
MG	machine gun
MiD	Mentioned in Despatches
Mk	Mark (ie version)
MRAF	Marshal of the RAF
msg	message
mt	motor
MU	maintenance unit
NCO	non-commissioned officer
NEAF	Near East Air Force
NF	night fighter
NFS	National Fire Service
NTR	nothing to report
obj	objective
OCU	Operational Conversion Unit
OP	observation post, operation
OR	other rank
ORB	Operations Record Book
ORBAT	Order of battle
para	parachute
pdr	pounder (artillery)

PFF	Pathfinder Force
pl	platoon
pm	provost marshal
PMRAFNS	Princess Mary's RAF Nursing Service
pnr	pioneer
PO/P/O, Plt Off	pilot officer
POL	petrol, oil, lubricants
PoW	Prisoner of War
pte	private
ptl	petrol
PWE	Political Warfare Executive
QM	quarter master
QMS	quarter master sergeant
RA	Royal Artillery
RAAF	Royal Australian Air Force
RCAF	Royal Canadian Air Force
RADAR	Radio Direction and Ranging
RAFVR	RAF Volunteer Reserve
RDF	Radio Direction Finding (radar)
RE	Royal Engineers
recce	reconnaissance
regt	regiment
rf	radio frequency
RFA	Royal Fleet Auxiliary
rfm	rifleman
RM	Royal Marines
RN	Royal Navy
RNR	Royal Naval Reserve
RNVR	Royal Naval Volunteer Reserve
RNZAF	Royal New Zealand Air Force
ROC	Royal Observer Corps
RSM	Regimental Sergeant Major
RSU	Repair and Salvage Unit
RV	rendezvous
S/L, S/Ldr, Sqd Ldr	Squadron Leader
SAA	small arms ammunition
SAAF	South African Air Force
SAC	Senior Aircraftsman
SDF	special duties flight
SEAC	South East Asia Command

sec	section
sgt	sergeant
SHAEF	Supreme Headquarters Allied Expeditionary Force
sig, sgl	signal
SIO	Senior Intelligence Officer
SIU	Signal Intelligence Unit
SL	searchlight, start line
SOE	Special Operations Executive
SP	self-propelled mounting, starting point
sp	support
spr	sapper
sqn, sqdn	squadron
SRO	Station Routing Orders
str	strength
SU	Signals Unit
svy	survey
TA	Territorial Army
tbc	to be confirmed
tbd	to be decided
TC	Transport Command
tech	technical
TF	training flight
TI	Target Indicator
tk	tank
TOC	taken on charge
TOPSEC	top secret
tp(s)	troops(s)
tpr	trooper
tpt	transport
UAS	University Air Squadron
uxb	unexploded bomb
VAD	Volunteer Aid Detachment (nursing)
VE	Victory in Europe
veh	vehicle
VJ	Victory in Japan
W/C, W/Cdr	Wing Commander
W/T	wireless telegraphy
WAAC	Women's Army Auxiliary Corps
WAAF	Women's Auxiliary Air Force
WD	War Department

wef	with immediate effect
WI	wireless interception
WIA	wounded in action
WLA	Women's Land Army
wksp	workshop
WO	warrant officer
WOP	wireless operator
WOP/AG	wireless operator/air gunner
wpn	weapon
WRN	Women's Royal Navy (WRENS)
WSAO	Weekly summary of air operations
wx	weather

Sources: Ken Delve, *The Source Book of the RAF* (Airlife Publishing, 1994); George Forty, *British Army Handbook 1939-1945* (Sutton, 1998); www.secondworldwar.co.uk.

Appendix IV

STATISTICS OF THE WAR

These statistics may help put the war and the tremendous impact it had on millions of people into context. The abbreviation n/k means not known.

Table 1   **Population and numbers served in forces**

Country	Population (1939)	Number served in forces
Australia	6.9m	1.34m
Canada	11.1m	1.1m
France	42m	4m[1]
Germany	78m	17.9m
India	359m	2.582m
Italy	43.8m	n/k
Japan	72.2m	9.1m
New Zealand	1.6m	n/k
Poland	34.8m	1.2m[2]
UK	47.5m	5.896m
USA	129.2m	16.354m
USSR	194.1m	c30m

[1] In 1940, plus 600,000 in Free French forces
[2] In 1939, plus c90,000 in Western Europe, 200,000 with Russians

Source: John Ellis, *The World War II Databook* (Aurum Press, 1993), pp253-4.

Table 2   **Military and civilian casualties**

Country	Forces casualties			Civilian casualties
	Killed and missing	*Wounded*	*Prisoners of war*	
Australia	294,000	398,000	264,000	
Canada	39,300	53,200	9,000	
France	c122,000	335,000	1,456,500	470,000
Germany	3,250,000	4,606,600	n/k	2,350,000
India	36,100	64,300	79,500	300,000
Italy	226,900	n/k	n/k	60,000
Japan	1,740,000	94,000	41,000	685,400
New Zealand	12,200	19,300	8,500	
Poland	c90,500	c166,700	c787,000	5,300,000
UK	305,800	277,100	172,600	146,800
USA	405,400	670,800	139,700	
USSR	11,000,000	n/k	c6,000,000	6,700,000

Source: John Ellis, *The World War II Databook* (Aurum Press, 1993), pp253-4.

Table 3   **Battle casualties by service**

Country	Service	No served	Killed/ Missing	Wounded	PoW
USA	Army	c7,900,000	165,800	574,300	79,700
	Air Force	c34,400,000	54,700	17,900	40,200
	Navy	4,183,000	36,900	37,800	n/k
	Marines	669,000	19,600	67,200	n/k
UK	Army[1]	3,778,000	177,800	239,600	152,076
	RAF[2]	1,185,000	76,300	22,800	13,100
	RN[3]	923,000	51,600	14,700	7,400
Germany	Army	c13,000,000	1,622,600	4,188,000	1,646,300
	Luftwaffe	c3,400,000	294,000	216,600	n/k
	Navy	c1,150,000	149,200	25,300	n/k
Japan	Army	c6,300,000	1,526,000	85,600	41,500
	Navy	c2,100,000	414,900	8,900	*(inc in Army figs)*

No figures for Russian forces available.

Notes
[1] Of whom 2,640,000 served overseas.
[2] Bomber Command losses were 59,423 killed or missing out of 125,000 served; a mortality rate of 47.5% (the highest proportion endured by any higher formation on either side).
[3] Not including the Merchant Navy, whose casualties were 34,902 killed and missing, 4,707 wounded and 5,720 PoWs.

Source: John Ellis, *The World War II Databook* (Aurum Press, 1993), p254.

Table 4   Military manpower raised by United Kingdom

	On entry into war	At end of war	Total mobilised	% of total mobilised
Army	402,000	2,931,000	3,778,000	64
Royal Air Force	118,000	963,000	1,185,000	20
Royal Navy	161,000	789,000	923,000	16
Armed forces	681,000	4,683,000	5,896,000	100

Adapted from John Ellis, *The World War II Databook* (Aurum Press, 1993), p228.

Table 5   Prisoners and casualties in the war against Japan

The numbers of Allied prisoners in South East Asia and the Far East were:	
United Kingdom	50,016
Australian	21,000
American	26,942
Dutch	18,000
Canadian	2,018
Indian	14,000
French Indo China	n/k

Of the 50,016 total United Kingdom forces captured: 42,610 were Army of whom 10,298 were killed or died in captivity; 5,102 were RAF of whom 1,714 were killed or died in captivity; 2,304 were Royal Navy of whom 421 were killed or died in captivity. In total 12,433 (25%) of British PoWs were killed or died while in the camps.

Source: www.cofoe.org.uk, based on an unidentified official publication of 1946.

INDEX